C-945 CAREER EXAMINATION SERIES

This is your
PASSBOOK for...

Civil Engineering Trainee

Test Preparation Study Guide
Questions & Answers

COPYRIGHT NOTICE

This book is SOLELY intended for, is sold ONLY to, and its use is RESTRICTED to individual, bona fide applicants or candidates who qualify by virtue of having seriously filed applications for appropriate license, certificate, professional and/or promotional advancement, higher school matriculation, scholarship, or other legitimate requirements of education and/or governmental authorities.

This book is NOT intended for use, class instruction, tutoring, training, duplication, copying, reprinting, excerption, or adaptation, etc., by:

1) Other publishers
2) Proprietors and/or Instructors of "Coaching" and/or Preparatory Courses
3) Personnel and/or Training Divisions of commercial, industrial, and governmental organizations
4) Schools, colleges, or universities and/or their departments and staffs, including teachers and other personnel
5) Testing Agencies or Bureaus
6) Study groups which seek by the purchase of a single volume to copy and/or duplicate and/or adapt this material for use by the group as a whole without having purchased individual volumes for each of the members of the group
7) Et al.

Such persons would be in violation of appropriate Federal and State statutes.

PROVISION OF LICENSING AGREEMENTS – Recognized educational, commercial, industrial, and governmental institutions and organizations, and others legitimately engaged in educational pursuits, including training, testing, and measurement activities, may address request for a licensing agreement to the copyright owners, who will determine whether, and under what conditions, including fees and charges, the materials in this book may be used them. In other words, a licensing facility exists for the legitimate use of the material in this book on other than an individual basis. However, it is asseverated and affirmed here that the material in this book CANNOT be used without the receipt of the express permission of such a licensing agreement from the Publishers. Inquiries re licensing should be addressed to the company, attention rights and permissions department.

All rights reserved, including the right of reproduction in whole or in part, in any form or by any means, electronic or mechanical, including photocopying, recording, or by any information storage and retrieval system, without permission in writing from the Publisher.

Copyright © 2024 by
National Learning Corporation

212 Michael Drive, Syosset, NY 11791
(516) 921-8888 • www.passbooks.com
E-mail: info@passbooks.com

PUBLISHED IN THE UNITED STATES OF AMERICA

PASSBOOK® SERIES

THE *PASSBOOK® SERIES* has been created to prepare applicants and candidates for the ultimate academic battlefield – the examination room.

At some time in our lives, each and every one of us may be required to take an examination – for validation, matriculation, admission, qualification, registration, certification, or licensure.

Based on the assumption that every applicant or candidate has met the basic formal educational standards, has taken the required number of courses, and read the necessary texts, the *PASSBOOK® SERIES* furnishes the one special preparation which may assure passing with confidence, instead of failing with insecurity. Examination questions – together with answers – are furnished as the basic vehicle for study so that the mysteries of the examination and its compounding difficulties may be eliminated or diminished by a sure method.

This book is meant to help you pass your examination provided that you qualify and are serious in your objective.

The entire field is reviewed through the huge store of content information which is succinctly presented through a provocative and challenging approach – the question-and-answer method.

A climate of success is established by furnishing the correct answers at the end of each test.

You soon learn to recognize types of questions, forms of questions, and patterns of questioning. You may even begin to anticipate expected outcomes.

You perceive that many questions are repeated or adapted so that you can gain acute insights, which may enable you to score many sure points.

You learn how to confront new questions, or types of questions, and to attack them confidently and work out the correct answers.

You note objectives and emphases, and recognize pitfalls and dangers, so that you may make positive educational adjustments.

Moreover, you are kept fully informed in relation to new concepts, methods, practices, and directions in the field.

You discover that you are actually taking the examination all the time: you are preparing for the examination by "taking" an examination, not by reading extraneous and/or supererogatory textbooks.

In short, this PASSBOOK®, used directedly, should be an important factor in helping you to pass your test.

CIVIL ENGINEERING TRAINEE

DUTIES AND RESPONSIBILITIES
Under direct supervision, performs elementary civil engineering work in the field, office or laboratory on the Junior Civil Engineer level, and receives a course of training in engineering work of moderate difficulty and responsibility on the Assistant Civil Engineer level. The work and training may be in one or more of the following engineering areas: development, design, construction, inspection, operations, maintenance, etc. Performs related work.

EXAMPLES OF TYPICAL TASKS
Assists in research, investigations, studies or examinations related to the civil engineering functions or activities of a department or agency. Assists in the preparation of maps, plans, drawings, specifications and estimates of quantities. Makes, traces, inks and letters drawings of acceptable standard quality. Uses, adjusts and maintains engineering instruments and equipment. Participates in field survey operations by acting as instrumentman, axeman, rodman, chainman or, when necessary, as chief of party on-routine surveys. Plots data on field note sheets. Inspects installations, material and equipment, performing tests to determine whether specifications, plans, contracts and standards of good workmanship have been adhered to. Assembles data, maintains files, keeps records and prepares reports. Receives training in such tasks as: supervising a small squad, unit or group engaged in the performance of elementary civil engineering work; engaging in research, investigations, studies or examinations related to the engineering functions or activities of a department or agency; preparing maps, plans, drawings, specifications; making computations, estimating costs, materials and labor requirements; participating in, and/or supervising the inspection of premises, installations, material and equipment to assure adherence to specifications, plans, contracts and standards of good workmanship.

HOW TO TAKE A TEST

I. YOU MUST PASS AN EXAMINATION

A. WHAT EVERY CANDIDATE SHOULD KNOW

Examination applicants often ask us for help in preparing for the written test. What can I study in advance? What kinds of questions will be asked? How will the test be given? How will the papers be graded?

As an applicant for a civil service examination, you may be wondering about some of these things. Our purpose here is to suggest effective methods of advance study and to describe civil service examinations.

Your chances for success on this examination can be increased if you know how to prepare. Those "pre-examination jitters" can be reduced if you know what to expect. You can even experience an adventure in good citizenship if you know why civil service exams are given.

B. WHY ARE CIVIL SERVICE EXAMINATIONS GIVEN?

Civil service examinations are important to you in two ways. As a citizen, you want public jobs filled by employees who know how to do their work. As a job seeker, you want a fair chance to compete for that job on an equal footing with other candidates. The best-known means of accomplishing this two-fold goal is the competitive examination.

Exams are widely publicized throughout the nation. They may be administered for jobs in federal, state, city, municipal, town or village governments or agencies.

Any citizen may apply, with some limitations, such as the age or residence of applicants. Your experience and education may be reviewed to see whether you meet the requirements for the particular examination. When these requirements exist, they are reasonable and applied consistently to all applicants. Thus, a competitive examination may cause you some uneasiness now, but it is your privilege and safeguard.

C. HOW ARE CIVIL SERVICE EXAMS DEVELOPED?

Examinations are carefully written by trained technicians who are specialists in the field known as "psychological measurement," in consultation with recognized authorities in the field of work that the test will cover. These experts recommend the subject matter areas or skills to be tested; only those knowledges or skills important to your success on the job are included. The most reliable books and source materials available are used as references. Together, the experts and technicians judge the difficulty level of the questions.

Test technicians know how to phrase questions so that the problem is clearly stated. Their ethics do not permit "trick" or "catch" questions. Questions may have been tried out on sample groups, or subjected to statistical analysis, to determine their usefulness.

Written tests are often used in combination with performance tests, ratings of training and experience, and oral interviews. All of these measures combine to form the best-known means of finding the right person for the right job.

II. HOW TO PASS THE WRITTEN TEST

A. NATURE OF THE EXAMINATION

To prepare intelligently for civil service examinations, you should know how they differ from school examinations you have taken. In school you were assigned certain definite pages to read or subjects to cover. The examination questions were quite detailed and usually emphasized memory. Civil service exams, on the other hand, try to discover your present ability to perform the duties of a position, plus your potentiality to learn these duties. In other words, a civil service exam attempts to predict how successful you will be. Questions cover such a broad area that they cannot be as minute and detailed as school exam questions.

In the public service similar kinds of work, or positions, are grouped together in one "class." This process is known as *position-classification*. All the positions in a class are paid according to the salary range for that class. One class title covers all of these positions, and they are all tested by the same examination.

B. FOUR BASIC STEPS

1) Study the announcement

How, then, can you know what subjects to study? Our best answer is: "Learn as much as possible about the class of positions for which you've applied." The exam will test the knowledge, skills and abilities needed to do the work.

Your most valuable source of information about the position you want is the official exam announcement. This announcement lists the training and experience qualifications. Check these standards and apply only if you come reasonably close to meeting them.

The brief description of the position in the examination announcement offers some clues to the subjects which will be tested. Think about the job itself. Review the duties in your mind. Can you perform them, or are there some in which you are rusty? Fill in the blank spots in your preparation.

Many jurisdictions preview the written test in the exam announcement by including a section called "Knowledge and Abilities Required," "Scope of the Examination," or some similar heading. Here you will find out specifically what fields will be tested.

2) Review your own background

Once you learn in general what the position is all about, and what you need to know to do the work, ask yourself which subjects you already know fairly well and which need improvement. You may wonder whether to concentrate on improving your strong areas or on building some background in your fields of weakness. When the announcement has specified "some knowledge" or "considerable knowledge," or has used adjectives like "beginning principles of..." or "advanced ... methods," you can get a clue as to the number and difficulty of questions to be asked in any given field. More questions, and hence broader coverage, would be included for those subjects which are more important in the work. Now weigh your strengths and weaknesses against the job requirements and prepare accordingly.

3) Determine the level of the position

Another way to tell how intensively you should prepare is to understand the level of the job for which you are applying. Is it the entering level? In other words, is this the position in which beginners in a field of work are hired? Or is it an intermediate or advanced level? Sometimes this is indicated by such words as "Junior" or "Senior" in the class title. Other jurisdictions use Roman numerals to designate the level – Clerk I, Clerk II, for example. The word "Supervisor" sometimes appears in the title. If the level is not indicated by the title, check the description of duties. Will you be working under very close supervision, or will you have responsibility for independent decisions in this work?

4) Choose appropriate study materials

Now that you know the subjects to be examined and the relative amount of each subject to be covered, you can choose suitable study materials. For beginning level jobs, or even advanced ones, if you have a pronounced weakness in some aspect of your training, read a modern, standard textbook in that field. Be sure it is up to date and has general coverage. Such books are normally available at your library, and the librarian will be glad to help you locate one. For entry-level positions, questions of appropriate difficulty are chosen -- neither highly advanced questions, nor those too simple. Such questions require careful thought but not advanced training.

If the position for which you are applying is technical or advanced, you will read more advanced, specialized material. If you are already familiar with the basic principles of your field, elementary textbooks would waste your time. Concentrate on advanced textbooks and technical periodicals. Think through the concepts and review difficult problems in your field.

These are all general sources. You can get more ideas on your own initiative, following these leads. For example, training manuals and publications of the government agency which employs workers in your field can be useful, particularly for technical and professional positions. A letter or visit to the government department involved may result in more specific study suggestions, and certainly will provide you with a more definite idea of the exact nature of the position you are seeking.

III. KINDS OF TESTS

Tests are used for purposes other than measuring knowledge and ability to perform specified duties. For some positions, it is equally important to test ability to make adjustments to new situations or to profit from training. In others, basic mental abilities not dependent on information are essential. Questions which test these things may not appear as pertinent to the duties of the position as those which test for knowledge and information. Yet they are often highly important parts of a fair examination. For very general questions, it is almost impossible to help you direct your study efforts. What we can do is to point out some of the more common of these general abilities needed in public service positions and describe some typical questions.

1) General information

Broad, general information has been found useful for predicting job success in some kinds of work. This is tested in a variety of ways, from vocabulary lists to questions about current events. Basic background in some field of work, such as sociology or economics, may be sampled in a group of questions. Often these are principles which have become familiar to most persons through exposure rather than through formal training. It is difficult to advise you how to study for these questions; being alert to the world around you is our best suggestion.

2) Verbal ability

An example of an ability needed in many positions is verbal or language ability. Verbal ability is, in brief, the ability to use and understand words. Vocabulary and grammar tests are typical measures of this ability. Reading comprehension or paragraph interpretation questions are common in many kinds of civil service tests. You are given a paragraph of written material and asked to find its central meaning.

3) Numerical ability

Number skills can be tested by the familiar arithmetic problem, by checking paired lists of numbers to see which are alike and which are different, or by interpreting charts and graphs. In the latter test, a graph may be printed in the test booklet which you are asked to use as the basis for answering questions.

4) Observation

A popular test for law-enforcement positions is the observation test. A picture is shown to you for several minutes, then taken away. Questions about the picture test your ability to observe both details and larger elements.

5) Following directions

In many positions in the public service, the employee must be able to carry out written instructions dependably and accurately. You may be given a chart with several columns, each column listing a variety of information. The questions require you to carry out directions involving the information given in the chart.

6) Skills and aptitudes

Performance tests effectively measure some manual skills and aptitudes. When the skill is one in which you are trained, such as typing or shorthand, you can practice. These tests are often very much like those given in business school or high school courses. For many of the other skills and aptitudes, however, no short-time preparation can be made. Skills and abilities natural to you or that you have developed throughout your lifetime are being tested.

Many of the general questions just described provide all the data needed to answer the questions and ask you to use your reasoning ability to find the answers. Your best preparation for these tests, as well as for tests of facts and ideas, is to be at your physical and mental best. You, no doubt, have your own methods of getting into an exam-taking mood and keeping "in shape." The next section lists some ideas on this subject.

IV. KINDS OF QUESTIONS

Only rarely is the "essay" question, which you answer in narrative form, used in civil service tests. Civil service tests are usually of the short-answer type. Full instructions for answering these questions will be given to you at the examination. But in case this is your first experience with short-answer questions and separate answer sheets, here is what you need to know:

1) Multiple-choice Questions

Most popular of the short-answer questions is the "multiple choice" or "best answer" question. It can be used, for example, to test for factual knowledge, ability to solve problems or judgment in meeting situations found at work.

A multiple-choice question is normally one of three types—
- It can begin with an incomplete statement followed by several possible endings. You are to find the one ending which *best* completes the statement, although some of the others may not be entirely wrong.
- It can also be a complete statement in the form of a question which is answered by choosing one of the statements listed.

- It can be in the form of a problem – again you select the best answer.

Here is an example of a multiple-choice question with a discussion which should give you some clues as to the method for choosing the right answer:

When an employee has a complaint about his assignment, the action which will *best* help him overcome his difficulty is to
- A. discuss his difficulty with his coworkers
- B. take the problem to the head of the organization
- C. take the problem to the person who gave him the assignment
- D. say nothing to anyone about his complaint

In answering this question, you should study each of the choices to find which is best. Consider choice "A" – Certainly an employee may discuss his complaint with fellow employees, but no change or improvement can result, and the complaint remains unresolved. Choice "B" is a poor choice since the head of the organization probably does not know what assignment you have been given, and taking your problem to him is known as "going over the head" of the supervisor. The supervisor, or person who made the assignment, is the person who can clarify it or correct any injustice. Choice "C" is, therefore, correct. To say nothing, as in choice "D," is unwise. Supervisors have and interest in knowing the problems employees are facing, and the employee is seeking a solution to his problem.

2) True/False Questions

The "true/false" or "right/wrong" form of question is sometimes used. Here a complete statement is given. Your job is to decide whether the statement is right or wrong.

SAMPLE: A roaming cell-phone call to a nearby city costs less than a non-roaming call to a distant city.

This statement is wrong, or false, since roaming calls are more expensive.

This is not a complete list of all possible question forms, although most of the others are variations of these common types. You will always get complete directions for answering questions. Be sure you understand *how* to mark your answers – ask questions until you do.

V. RECORDING YOUR ANSWERS

Computer terminals are used more and more today for many different kinds of exams.

For an examination with very few applicants, you may be told to record your answers in the test booklet itself. Separate answer sheets are much more common. If this separate answer sheet is to be scored by machine – and this is often the case – it is highly important that you mark your answers correctly in order to get credit.

An electronic scoring machine is often used in civil service offices because of the speed with which papers can be scored. Machine-scored answer sheets must be marked with a pencil, which will be given to you. This pencil has a high graphite content which responds to the electronic scoring machine. As a matter of fact, stray dots may register as answers, so do not let your pencil rest on the answer sheet while you are pondering the correct answer. Also, if your pencil lead breaks or is otherwise defective, ask for another.

Since the answer sheet will be dropped in a slot in the scoring machine, be careful not to bend the corners or get the paper crumpled.

The answer sheet normally has five vertical columns of numbers, with 30 numbers to a column. These numbers correspond to the question numbers in your test booklet. After each number, going across the page are four or five pairs of dotted lines. These short dotted lines have small letters or numbers above them. The first two pairs may also have a "T" or "F" above the letters. This indicates that the first two pairs only are to be used if the questions are of the true-false type. If the questions are multiple choice, disregard the "T" and "F" and pay attention only to the small letters or numbers.

Answer your questions in the manner of the sample that follows:

32. The largest city in the United States is
    A. Washington, D.C.
    B. New York City
    C. Chicago
    D. Detroit
    E. San Francisco

1) Choose the answer you think is best. (New York City is the largest, so "B" is correct.)
2) Find the row of dotted lines numbered the same as the question you are answering. (Find row number 32)
3) Find the pair of dotted lines corresponding to the answer. (Find the pair of lines under the mark "B.")
4) Make a solid black mark between the dotted lines.

VI. BEFORE THE TEST

Common sense will help you find procedures to follow to get ready for an examination. Too many of us, however, overlook these sensible measures. Indeed, nervousness and fatigue have been found to be the most serious reasons why applicants fail to do their best on civil service tests. Here is a list of reminders:

- Begin your preparation early – Don't wait until the last minute to go scurrying around for books and materials or to find out what the position is all about.
- Prepare continuously – An hour a night for a week is better than an all-night cram session. This has been definitely established. What is more, a night a week for a month will return better dividends than crowding your study into a shorter period of time.
- Locate the place of the exam – You have been sent a notice telling you when and where to report for the examination. If the location is in a different town or otherwise unfamiliar to you, it would be well to inquire the best route and learn something about the building.
- Relax the night before the test – Allow your mind to rest. Do not study at all that night. Plan some mild recreation or diversion; then go to bed early and get a good night's sleep.
- Get up early enough to make a leisurely trip to the place for the test – This way unforeseen events, traffic snarls, unfamiliar buildings, etc. will not upset you.
- Dress comfortably – A written test is not a fashion show. You will be known by number and not by name, so wear something comfortable.

- Leave excess paraphernalia at home – Shopping bags and odd bundles will get in your way. You need bring only the items mentioned in the official notice you received; usually everything you need is provided. Do not bring reference books to the exam. They will only confuse those last minutes and be taken away from you when in the test room.
- Arrive somewhat ahead of time – If because of transportation schedules you must get there very early, bring a newspaper or magazine to take your mind off yourself while waiting.
- Locate the examination room – When you have found the proper room, you will be directed to the seat or part of the room where you will sit. Sometimes you are given a sheet of instructions to read while you are waiting. Do not fill out any forms until you are told to do so; just read them and be prepared.
- Relax and prepare to listen to the instructions
- If you have any physical problem that may keep you from doing your best, be sure to tell the test administrator. If you are sick or in poor health, you really cannot do your best on the exam. You can come back and take the test some other time.

VII. AT THE TEST

The day of the test is here and you have the test booklet in your hand. The temptation to get going is very strong. Caution! There is more to success than knowing the right answers. You must know how to identify your papers and understand variations in the type of short-answer question used in this particular examination. Follow these suggestions for maximum results from your efforts:

1) Cooperate with the monitor

The test administrator has a duty to create a situation in which you can be as much at ease as possible. He will give instructions, tell you when to begin, check to see that you are marking your answer sheet correctly, and so on. He is not there to guard you, although he will see that your competitors do not take unfair advantage. He wants to help you do your best.

2) Listen to all instructions

Don't jump the gun! Wait until you understand all directions. In most civil service tests you get more time than you need to answer the questions. So don't be in a hurry. Read each word of instructions until you clearly understand the meaning. Study the examples, listen to all announcements and follow directions. Ask questions if you do not understand what to do.

3) Identify your papers

Civil service exams are usually identified by number only. You will be assigned a number; you must not put your name on your test papers. Be sure to copy your number correctly. Since more than one exam may be given, copy your exact examination title.

4) Plan your time

Unless you are told that a test is a "speed" or "rate of work" test, speed itself is usually not important. Time enough to answer all the questions will be provided, but this does not mean that you have all day. An overall time limit has been set. Divide the total time (in minutes) by the number of questions to determine the approximate time you have for each question.

5) Do not linger over difficult questions

If you come across a difficult question, mark it with a paper clip (useful to have along) and come back to it when you have been through the booklet. One caution if you do this – be sure to skip a number on your answer sheet as well. Check often to be sure that you have not lost your place and that you are marking in the row numbered the same as the question you are answering.

6) Read the questions

Be sure you know what the question asks! Many capable people are unsuccessful because they failed to *read* the questions correctly.

7) Answer all questions

Unless you have been instructed that a penalty will be deducted for incorrect answers, it is better to guess than to omit a question.

8) Speed tests

It is often better NOT to guess on speed tests. It has been found that on timed tests people are tempted to spend the last few seconds before time is called in marking answers at random – without even reading them – in the hope of picking up a few extra points. To discourage this practice, the instructions may warn you that your score will be "corrected" for guessing. That is, a penalty will be applied. The incorrect answers will be deducted from the correct ones, or some other penalty formula will be used.

9) Review your answers

If you finish before time is called, go back to the questions you guessed or omitted to give them further thought. Review other answers if you have time.

10) Return your test materials

If you are ready to leave before others have finished or time is called, take ALL your materials to the monitor and leave quietly. Never take any test material with you. The monitor can discover whose papers are not complete, and taking a test booklet may be grounds for disqualification.

VIII. EXAMINATION TECHNIQUES

1) Read the general instructions carefully. These are usually printed on the first page of the exam booklet. As a rule, these instructions refer to the timing of the examination; the fact that you should not start work until the signal and must stop work at a signal, etc. If there are any *special* instructions, such as a choice of questions to be answered, make sure that you note this instruction carefully.

2) When you are ready to start work on the examination, that is as soon as the signal has been given, read the instructions to each question booklet, underline any key words or phrases, such as *least, best, outline, describe* and the like. In this way you will tend to answer as requested rather than discover on reviewing your paper that you *listed without describing*, that you selected the *worst* choice rather than the *best* choice, etc.

3) If the examination is of the objective or multiple-choice type – that is, each question will also give a series of possible answers: A, B, C or D, and you are called upon to select the best answer and write the letter next to that answer on your answer paper – it is advisable to start answering each question in turn. There may be anywhere from 50 to 100 such questions in the three or four hours allotted and you can see how much time would be taken if you read through all the questions before beginning to answer any. Furthermore, if you come across a question or group of questions which you know would be difficult to answer, it would undoubtedly affect your handling of all the other questions.

4) If the examination is of the essay type and contains but a few questions, it is a moot point as to whether you should read all the questions before starting to answer any one. Of course, if you are given a choice – say five out of seven and the like – then it is essential to read all the questions so you can eliminate the two that are most difficult. If, however, you are asked to answer all the questions, there may be danger in trying to answer the easiest one first because you may find that you will spend too much time on it. The best technique is to answer the first question, then proceed to the second, etc.

5) Time your answers. Before the exam begins, write down the time it started, then add the time allowed for the examination and write down the time it must be completed, then divide the time available somewhat as follows:
   - If 3-1/2 hours are allowed, that would be 210 minutes. If you have 80 objective-type questions, that would be an average of 2-1/2 minutes per question. Allow yourself no more than 2 minutes per question, or a total of 160 minutes, which will permit about 50 minutes to review.
   - If for the time allotment of 210 minutes there are 7 essay questions to answer, that would average about 30 minutes a question. Give yourself only 25 minutes per question so that you have about 35 minutes to review.

6) The most important instruction is to *read each question* and make sure you know what is wanted. The second most important instruction is to *time yourself properly* so that you answer every question. The third most important instruction is to *answer every question*. Guess if you have to but include something for each question. Remember that you will receive no credit for a blank and will probably receive some credit if you write something in answer to an essay question. If you guess a letter – say "B" for a multiple-choice question – you may have guessed right. If you leave a blank as an answer to a multiple-choice question, the examiners may respect your feelings but it will not add a point to your score. Some exams may penalize you for wrong answers, so in such cases *only*, you may not want to guess unless you have some basis for your answer.

7) Suggestions
   a. Objective-type questions
      1. Examine the question booklet for proper sequence of pages and questions
      2. Read all instructions carefully
      3. Skip any question which seems too difficult; return to it after all other questions have been answered
      4. Apportion your time properly; do not spend too much time on any single question or group of questions

5. Note and underline key words – *all, most, fewest, least, best, worst, same, opposite*, etc.
6. Pay particular attention to negatives
7. Note unusual option, e.g., unduly long, short, complex, different or similar in content to the body of the question
8. Observe the use of "hedging" words – *probably, may, most likely*, etc.
9. Make sure that your answer is put next to the same number as the question
10. Do not second-guess unless you have good reason to believe the second answer is definitely more correct
11. Cross out original answer if you decide another answer is more accurate; do not erase until you are ready to hand your paper in
12. Answer all questions; guess unless instructed otherwise
13. Leave time for review

   b. Essay questions
1. Read each question carefully
2. Determine exactly what is wanted. Underline key words or phrases.
3. Decide on outline or paragraph answer
4. Include many different points and elements unless asked to develop any one or two points or elements
5. Show impartiality by giving pros and cons unless directed to select one side only
6. Make and write down any assumptions you find necessary to answer the questions
7. Watch your English, grammar, punctuation and choice of words
8. Time your answers; don't crowd material

8) Answering the essay question

Most essay questions can be answered by framing the specific response around several key words or ideas. Here are a few such key words or ideas:

M's: manpower, materials, methods, money, management
P's: purpose, program, policy, plan, procedure, practice, problems, pitfalls, personnel, public relations

   a. Six basic steps in handling problems:
1. Preliminary plan and background development
2. Collect information, data and facts
3. Analyze and interpret information, data and facts
4. Analyze and develop solutions as well as make recommendations
5. Prepare report and sell recommendations
6. Install recommendations and follow up effectiveness

   b. Pitfalls to avoid
1. *Taking things for granted* – A statement of the situation does not necessarily imply that each of the elements is necessarily true; for example, a complaint may be invalid and biased so that all that can be taken for granted is that a complaint has been registered

2. *Considering only one side of a situation* – Wherever possible, indicate several alternatives and then point out the reasons you selected the best one
3. *Failing to indicate follow up* – Whenever your answer indicates action on your part, make certain that you will take proper follow-up action to see how successful your recommendations, procedures or actions turn out to be
4. *Taking too long in answering any single question* – Remember to time your answers properly

IX. AFTER THE TEST

Scoring procedures differ in detail among civil service jurisdictions although the general principles are the same. Whether the papers are hand-scored or graded by machine we have described, they are nearly always graded by number. That is, the person who marks the paper knows only the number – never the name – of the applicant. Not until all the papers have been graded will they be matched with names. If other tests, such as training and experience or oral interview ratings have been given, scores will be combined. Different parts of the examination usually have different weights. For example, the written test might count 60 percent of the final grade, and a rating of training and experience 40 percent. In many jurisdictions, veterans will have a certain number of points added to their grades.

After the final grade has been determined, the names are placed in grade order and an eligible list is established. There are various methods for resolving ties between those who get the same final grade – probably the most common is to place first the name of the person whose application was received first. Job offers are made from the eligible list in the order the names appear on it. You will be notified of your grade and your rank as soon as all these computations have been made. This will be done as rapidly as possible.

People who are found to meet the requirements in the announcement are called "eligibles." Their names are put on a list of eligible candidates. An eligible's chances of getting a job depend on how high he stands on this list and how fast agencies are filling jobs from the list.

When a job is to be filled from a list of eligibles, the agency asks for the names of people on the list of eligibles for that job. When the civil service commission receives this request, it sends to the agency the names of the three people highest on this list. Or, if the job to be filled has specialized requirements, the office sends the agency the names of the top three persons who meet these requirements from the general list.

The appointing officer makes a choice from among the three people whose names were sent to him. If the selected person accepts the appointment, the names of the others are put back on the list to be considered for future openings.

That is the rule in hiring from all kinds of eligible lists, whether they are for typist, carpenter, chemist, or something else. For every vacancy, the appointing officer has his choice of any one of the top three eligibles on the list. This explains why the person whose name is on top of the list sometimes does not get an appointment when some of the persons lower on the list do. If the appointing officer chooses the second or third eligible, the No. 1 eligible does not get a job at once, but stays on the list until he is appointed or the list is terminated.

X. HOW TO PASS THE INTERVIEW TEST

The examination for which you applied requires an oral interview test. You have already taken the written test and you are now being called for the interview test – the final part of the formal examination.

You may think that it is not possible to prepare for an interview test and that there are no procedures to follow during an interview. Our purpose is to point out some things you can do in advance that will help you and some good rules to follow and pitfalls to avoid while you are being interviewed.

What is an interview supposed to test?

The written examination is designed to test the technical knowledge and competence of the candidate; the oral is designed to evaluate intangible qualities, not readily measured otherwise, and to establish a list showing the relative fitness of each candidate – as measured against his competitors – for the position sought. Scoring is not on the basis of "right" and "wrong," but on a sliding scale of values ranging from "not passable" to "outstanding." As a matter of fact, it is possible to achieve a relatively low score without a single "incorrect" answer because of evident weakness in the qualities being measured.

Occasionally, an examination may consist entirely of an oral test – either an individual or a group oral. In such cases, information is sought concerning the technical knowledges and abilities of the candidate, since there has been no written examination for this purpose. More commonly, however, an oral test is used to supplement a written examination.

Who conducts interviews?

The composition of oral boards varies among different jurisdictions. In nearly all, a representative of the personnel department serves as chairman. One of the members of the board may be a representative of the department in which the candidate would work. In some cases, "outside experts" are used, and, frequently, a businessman or some other representative of the general public is asked to serve. Labor and management or other special groups may be represented. The aim is to secure the services of experts in the appropriate field.

However the board is composed, it is a good idea (and not at all improper or unethical) to ascertain in advance of the interview who the members are and what groups they represent. When you are introduced to them, you will have some idea of their backgrounds and interests, and at least you will not stutter and stammer over their names.

What should be done before the interview?

While knowledge about the board members is useful and takes some of the surprise element out of the interview, there is other preparation which is more substantive. It *is* possible to prepare for an oral interview – in several ways:

1) Keep a copy of your application and review it carefully before the interview

This may be the only document before the oral board, and the starting point of the interview. Know what education and experience you have listed there, and the sequence and dates of all of it. Sometimes the board will ask you to review the highlights of your experience for them; you should not have to hem and haw doing it.

2) Study the class specification and the examination announcement

Usually, the oral board has one or both of these to guide them. The qualities, characteristics or knowledges required by the position sought are stated in these documents. They offer valuable clues as to the nature of the oral interview. For example, if the job involves supervisory responsibilities, the announcement will usually indicate that knowledge of modern supervisory methods and the qualifications of the candidate as a supervisor will be tested. If so, you can expect such questions, frequently in the form of a hypothetical situation which you are expected to solve. NEVER go into an oral without knowledge of the duties and responsibilities of the job you seek.

3) Think through each qualification required

Try to visualize the kind of questions you would ask if you were a board member. How well could you answer them? Try especially to appraise your own knowledge and background in each area, *measured against the job sought*, and identify any areas in which you are weak. Be critical and realistic – do not flatter yourself.

4) Do some general reading in areas in which you feel you may be weak

For example, if the job involves supervision and your past experience has NOT, some general reading in supervisory methods and practices, particularly in the field of human relations, might be useful. Do NOT study agency procedures or detailed manuals. The oral board will be testing your understanding and capacity, not your memory.

5) Get a good night's sleep and watch your general health and mental attitude

You will want a clear head at the interview. Take care of a cold or any other minor ailment, and of course, no hangovers.

What should be done on the day of the interview?

Now comes the day of the interview itself. Give yourself plenty of time to get there. Plan to arrive somewhat ahead of the scheduled time, particularly if your appointment is in the fore part of the day. If a previous candidate fails to appear, the board might be ready for you a bit early. By early afternoon an oral board is almost invariably behind schedule if there are many candidates, and you may have to wait. Take along a book or magazine to read, or your application to review, but leave any extraneous material in the waiting room when you go in for your interview. In any event, relax and compose yourself.

The matter of dress is important. The board is forming impressions about you – from your experience, your manners, your attitude, and your appearance. Give your personal appearance careful attention. Dress your best, but not your flashiest. Choose conservative, appropriate clothing, and be sure it is immaculate. This is a business interview, and your appearance should indicate that you regard it as such. Besides, being well groomed and properly dressed will help boost your confidence.

Sooner or later, someone will call your name and escort you into the interview room. *This is it.* From here on you are on your own. It is too late for any more preparation. But remember, you asked for this opportunity to prove your fitness, and you are here because your request was granted.

What happens when you go in?

The usual sequence of events will be as follows: The clerk (who is often the board stenographer) will introduce you to the chairman of the oral board, who will introduce you to the other members of the board. Acknowledge the introductions before you sit down. Do not be surprised if you find a microphone facing you or a stenotypist sitting by. Oral interviews are usually recorded in the event of an appeal or other review.

Usually the chairman of the board will open the interview by reviewing the highlights of your education and work experience from your application – primarily for the benefit of the other members of the board, as well as to get the material into the record. Do not interrupt or comment unless there is an error or significant misinterpretation; if that is the case, do not hesitate. But do not quibble about insignificant matters. Also, he will usually ask you some question about your education, experience or your present job – partly to get you to start talking and to establish the interviewing "rapport." He may start the actual questioning, or turn it over to one of the other members. Frequently, each member undertakes the questioning on a particular area, one in which he is perhaps most competent, so you can expect each member to participate in the examination. Because time is limited, you may also expect some rather abrupt switches in the direction the questioning takes, so do not be upset by it. Normally, a board member will not pursue a single line of questioning unless he discovers a particular strength or weakness.

After each member has participated, the chairman will usually ask whether any member has any further questions, then will ask you if you have anything you wish to add. Unless you are expecting this question, it may floor you. Worse, it may start you off on an extended, extemporaneous speech. The board is not usually seeking more information. The question is principally to offer you a last opportunity to present further qualifications or to indicate that you have nothing to add. So, if you feel that a significant qualification or characteristic has been overlooked, it is proper to point it out in a sentence or so. Do not compliment the board on the thoroughness of their examination – they have been sketchy, and you know it. If you wish, merely say, "No thank you, I have nothing further to add." This is a point where you can "talk yourself out" of a good impression or fail to present an important bit of information. Remember, *you close the interview yourself*.

The chairman will then say, "That is all, Mr. _____, thank you." Do not be startled; the interview is over, and quicker than you think. Thank him, gather your belongings and take your leave. Save your sigh of relief for the other side of the door.

How to put your best foot forward

Throughout this entire process, you may feel that the board individually and collectively is trying to pierce your defenses, seek out your hidden weaknesses and embarrass and confuse you. Actually, this is not true. They are obliged to make an appraisal of your qualifications for the job you are seeking, and they want to see you in your best light. Remember, they must interview all candidates and a non-cooperative candidate may become a failure in spite of their best efforts to bring out his qualifications. Here are 15 suggestions that will help you:

1) Be natural – Keep your attitude confident, not cocky

If you are not confident that you can do the job, do not expect the board to be. Do not apologize for your weaknesses, try to bring out your strong points. The board is interested in a positive, not negative, presentation. Cockiness will antagonize any board member and make him wonder if you are covering up a weakness by a false show of strength.

2) Get comfortable, but don't lounge or sprawl

Sit erectly but not stiffly. A careless posture may lead the board to conclude that you are careless in other things, or at least that you are not impressed by the importance of the occasion. Either conclusion is natural, even if incorrect. Do not fuss with your clothing, a pencil or an ashtray. Your hands may occasionally be useful to emphasize a point; do not let them become a point of distraction.

3) Do not wisecrack or make small talk

This is a serious situation, and your attitude should show that you consider it as such. Further, the time of the board is limited – they do not want to waste it, and neither should you.

4) Do not exaggerate your experience or abilities

In the first place, from information in the application or other interviews and sources, the board may know more about you than you think. Secondly, you probably will not get away with it. An experienced board is rather adept at spotting such a situation, so do not take the chance.

5) If you know a board member, do not make a point of it, yet do not hide it

Certainly you are not fooling him, and probably not the other members of the board. Do not try to take advantage of your acquaintanceship – it will probably do you little good.

6) Do not dominate the interview

Let the board do that. They will give you the clues – do not assume that you have to do all the talking. Realize that the board has a number of questions to ask you, and do not try to take up all the interview time by showing off your extensive knowledge of the answer to the first one.

7) Be attentive

You only have 20 minutes or so, and you should keep your attention at its sharpest throughout. When a member is addressing a problem or question to you, give him your undivided attention. Address your reply principally to him, but do not exclude the other board members.

8) Do not interrupt

A board member may be stating a problem for you to analyze. He will ask you a question when the time comes. Let him state the problem, and wait for the question.

9) Make sure you understand the question

Do not try to answer until you are sure what the question is. If it is not clear, restate it in your own words or ask the board member to clarify it for you. However, do not haggle about minor elements.

10) Reply promptly but not hastily

A common entry on oral board rating sheets is "candidate responded readily," or "candidate hesitated in replies." Respond as promptly and quickly as you can, but do not jump to a hasty, ill-considered answer.

11) Do not be peremptory in your answers

A brief answer is proper – but do not fire your answer back. That is a losing game from your point of view. The board member can probably ask questions much faster than you can answer them.

12) Do not try to create the answer you think the board member wants

He is interested in what kind of mind you have and how it works – not in playing games. Furthermore, he can usually spot this practice and will actually grade you down on it.

13) Do not switch sides in your reply merely to agree with a board member

Frequently, a member will take a contrary position merely to draw you out and to see if you are willing and able to defend your point of view. Do not start a debate, yet do not surrender a good position. If a position is worth taking, it is worth defending.

14) Do not be afraid to admit an error in judgment if you are shown to be wrong

The board knows that you are forced to reply without any opportunity for careful consideration. Your answer may be demonstrably wrong. If so, admit it and get on with the interview.

15) Do not dwell at length on your present job

The opening question may relate to your present assignment. Answer the question but do not go into an extended discussion. You are being examined for a *new* job, not your present one. As a matter of fact, try to phrase ALL your answers in terms of the job for which you are being examined.

Basis of Rating

Probably you will forget most of these "do's" and "don'ts" when you walk into the oral interview room. Even remembering them all will not ensure you a passing grade. Perhaps you did not have the qualifications in the first place. But remembering them will help you to put your best foot forward, without treading on the toes of the board members.

Rumor and popular opinion to the contrary notwithstanding, an oral board wants you to make the best appearance possible. They know you are under pressure – but they also want to see how you respond to it as a guide to what your reaction would be under the pressures of the job you seek. They will be influenced by the degree of poise you display, the personal traits you show and the manner in which you respond.

ABOUT THIS BOOK

This book contains tests divided into Examination Sections. Go through each test, answering every question in the margin. We have also attached a sample answer sheet at the back of the book that can be removed and used. At the end of each test look at the answer key and check your answers. On the ones you got wrong, look at the right answer choice and learn. Do not fill in the answers first. Do not memorize the questions and answers, but understand the answer and principles involved. On your test, the questions will likely be different from the samples. Questions are changed and new ones added. If you understand these past questions you should have success with any changes that arise. Tests may consist of several types of questions. We have additional books on each subject should more study be advisable or necessary for you. Finally, the more you study, the better prepared you will be. This book is intended to be the last thing you study before you walk into the examination room. Prior study of relevant texts is also recommended. NLC publishes some of these in our Fundamental Series. Knowledge and good sense are important factors in passing your exam. Good luck also helps. So now study this Passbook, absorb the material contained within and take that knowledge into the examination. Then do your best to pass that exam.

EXAMINATION SECTION

EXAMINATION SECTION
TEST 1

DIRECTIONS: Each question or incomplete statement is followed by several suggested answers or completions. Select the one that BEST answers the question or completes the statement. *PRINT THE LETTER OF THE CORRECT ANSWER IN THE SPACE AT THE RIGHT.*

1. In leveling, a backsight on BM *A* is 4.270 and the foresight on TP #1 is 7.384. The elevation of BM *A* is 27.842.
   The HI is

   A. 17.399   B. 32.112   C. 39.213   D. 43.764

   1.____

2. A bill of materials calls for twenty-four 4" x 10" x 16'0" wooden beams.
   The number of FBM in these beams is

   A. 1210   B. 1230   C. 1250   D. 1280

   2.____

3. Two kinds of concrete are being used in the construction of a reinforced concrete building. Slump tests show one concrete to have a slump of 7 inches, the other 3 inches. The concrete with the 7 inch slump would be used for

   A. beams   B. floors   C. roof   D. columns

   3.____

4. A planimeter is used to

   A. measure the area of plane figures
   B. draw parallel lines
   C. measure the distance between parallel lines
   D. measure distances on plans

   4.____

5. The bearing of line AB is N65°W, that of line AC is S15°E.
   The angle BAC is

   A. 130°   B. 120°   C. 75°   D. 45°

   5.____

6. In a right triangle, the hypotenuse, AB, is 13 feet long. The side AC is 12 feet and side BC is 5 feet long. A perpendicular is dropped from C to side AB.
   Its length, in feet, in MOST NEARLY

   A. 4.4   B. 4.6   C. 4.9   D. 5.1

   6.____

7. The roots of the equation $2x^2 - x - 15 = 0$ are

   A. -3.0, +2.5   B. +3.0, -5.0
   C. +1.5, -5.0   D. +3.0, -2.5

   7.____

8. In laying out a horizontal circular curve for a highway,

   A. the center of the curve must be located on the ground
   B. full stations are located by deflection angles and chord distances
   C. field taping must be done along the arc of the curve
   D. an Engineer's Level must be used

   8.____

9. In reinforced concrete construction, the reinforcing bars should be

   A. oiled to prevent rusting
   B. bent while at a red heat
   C. securely fastened so that they will not be displaced during the pour
   D. placed immediately after the concrete is poured

10. The distance between the zero and 100-foot marks of a steel tape is 99.9 feet. To lay out a true distance of 321.7 feet with this tape, the tape distance should be

    A. 319.7   B. 320.5   C. 322.0   D. 323.3

11.

   In which one of the cantilever retaining walls shown above is the main reinforcing steel, indicated by the dotted lines, CORRECTLY located?

   A. A   B. B   C. C   D. D

12. The sensitivity of a bubble tube such as those on a transit or that on a level is a function of the

    A. length of the bubble tube
    B. spacing of the graduations on the tube
    C. radius of curvature of the inner surface of the glass forming the top of the tube
    D. length of the bubble within the bubble tube

13. The water pressure at a point 175 feet below the surface is, in pounds per square inch, MOST NEARLY

    A. 76   B. 79   C. 82   D. 85

14. The sum of the interior angles of a five-sided polygon is

    A. 390°   B. 480°   C. 540°   D. 660°

15. A true meridian on a map indicates

    A. true north
    B. the equator
    C. the latitude
    D. the direction of the magnetic pole

16. Points A, B, and C lie on the circumference of a circle with a 10-inch radius. Angle BAC is 45°.
    The length of chord BC is, in inches, MOST NEARLY

    A. 8.1   B. 9.1   C. 14.1   D. 15.1

17. The equations of two straight lines are y = 2x + 4 and y = 6 - x.
    They coordinate of the point of intersection is MOST NEARLY

    A. 5.31   B. 5.33   C. 5.35   D. 5.39

18. Which of the following statements with respect to contour lines is NOT correct?

    A. Contours crossing streams form vees which point upstream.
    B. A closed contour represents a hill or depression.
    C. Contours never cross except in the case of an overhanging cliff.
    D. The horizontal distance between contours does not vary with the slope of the ground.

19. A bill of material calls for 2 x 4's, S4S. The dressed size of this lumber is, in inches,

    A. 3 x 5   B. 1 5/8 x 3 7/8   C. 1 3/8 x 3 5/8   D. 1 5/8 x 3 5/8

20. Of the following terms, the one which is LEAST related to the others is

    A. azimuth   B. camber   C. batter   D. grade

21. The larger the Modulus of elasticity of a material, the

    A. *greater* the stress it can withstand
    B. *greater* the strain it can withstand
    C. *less* it will be strained for a given stress
    D. *less* it will be stressed for a given strain

22. In a simple reinforced concrete beam in a building, the concrete below the reinforcing steel serves PRIMARILY

    A. as fire protection
    B. to increase the shearing strength of the beam
    C. to simplify construction
    D. to prevent rusting of the steel

23. The foot-pound is a unit of

    A. power   B. work   C. force   D. capacity

24. The resistance of a 60 watt 110 volt light bulb is MOST NEARLY, in ohms,

    A. 60   B. 110   C. 160   D. 200

25. A horizontal force of 45 pounds is applied to a 60-pound weight which is suspended by a wire.
    When the system is in equilibrium, the tension in the wire is, in pounds,

    A. 75   B. 80   C. 85   D. 90

KEY (CORRECT ANSWERS)

1. B
2. D
3. D
4. A
5. A

6. B
7. D
8. B
9. C
10. C

11. B
12. C
13. A
14. C
15. A

16. C
17. B
18. D
19. D
20. A

21. C
22. A
23. B
24. D
25. A

SOLUTIONS TO PROBLEMS

1. ANSWER: B
   The HI is independent of the foresight measurement.
   HI = 27.842 + 4.270 = 32.112

2. ANSWER: D
   One board ft. = 144 in.

   NO. of FBM = $\dfrac{(16 \times 12)(4)(10)(24)}{144}$ = 1280

5. ANSWER: A
   $\angle BAC$ = (90 - 65) + 90 + 15
          = 130

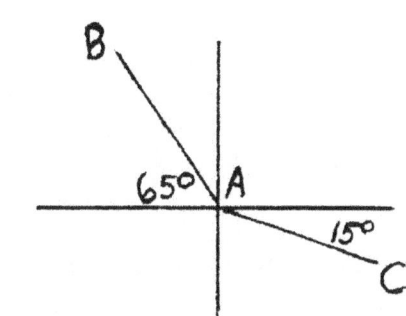

6. ANSWER: B
   sin B = 12/13 = y/5
   y = 60/13 = 4.6

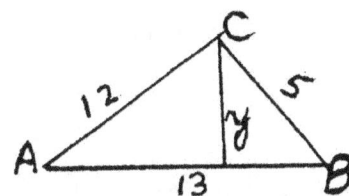

7. ANSWER: D
   (2x+5)(x-3) = 0
   x = -2.5; x = +3.0

10. ANSWER: C
    Error = 100 - 99.9 = 0.1 ft./100 ft. of true length
    ∴ 321.7 + 3(0.1) = 322.0 ft.

13. ANSWER: A
    One atmosphere (14.7 psi) = 34 ft. of water
    175/34 = 5.15 atm.
    (5.15)(14.7) = 76 psi.
    (This neglects the 1 atm. above the water surface.)

14. ANSWER: C
    For an n-sided polygon, the sum of the interior angles, say 2 a (for a regular polygon), is 2 an.
    2a = 180 - 360/n
    2na = 180n - 360 = 900 - 360 = 540° (for n=5)

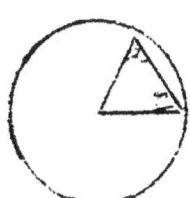

16. ANSWER: C
    $AB^2 = BC^2 + CA^2$
    $BC = CA$
    $2CB^2 = AB^2 = (20)^2 = 400"$
    $CB^2 = 400/2 = 200"$
    $CB = \sqrt{200} = 10\sqrt{2}$
    CB 14,14"

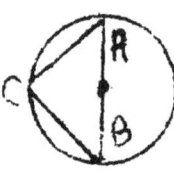

17. ANSWER: B
    $2x+4=6-x$; $x = 2/3$ at intersection
    $y = 2(2/3) + 4 = 5.33$

19. ANSWER: D
    According to American Lumber Standards, trimming of 2 x 4's to S4S means a 3/8 in. loss for each dimension.

21. ANSWER: C
    Modulus of elasticity = stress/strain. For a given stress, the strain decreases as the modulus increases.

23. ANSWER: B
    In general, work is force x distance.

24. ANSWER: D
    $P = VI = I^2R$
    $I = 60/110$; $R = V/I = (110)^2/60 \sim 200$

25. ANSWER: A
    The wire supports all the weight:
    T=75

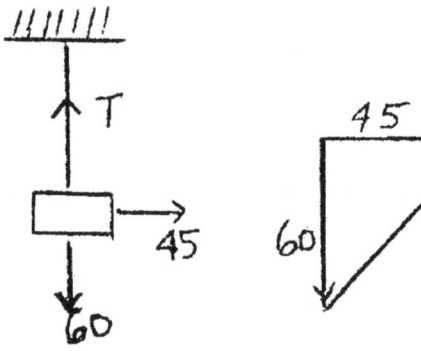

TEST 2

DIRECTIONS: Each question or incomplete statement is followed by several suggested answers or completions. Select the one that BEST answers the question or completes the statement. *PRINT THE LETTER OF THE CORRECT ANSWER IN THE SPACE AT THE RIGHT.*

1. A motor can raise a 3000-pound drop hammer with a velocity of 6 feet per second. Ignoring friction, the horsepower of the motor is

   A. 31.9   B. 32.7   C. 33.1   D. 34.3

2. In the system of pulleys shown at the right, the force F required to lift the 500 pound weight, ignoring friction, is MOST NEARLY.
   A. 990
   B. 450
   C. 250
   D. 100

3. A flask weighing 225 grams when empty weighs 446 grams when filled with water and 419 grams when filled with oil. The specific gravity of the oil is about

   A. 0.88   B. 0.91   C. 0.93   D. 0.95

4. Piles are NOT driven by

   A. steam hammer   B. drop hammer
   C. jack   D. water hammer

5. A protractor is used to

   A. measure area
   B. draw parallel lines
   C. draw guidelines for lettering
   D. measure or layout angles on a scale drawing

6. Partial payments totaling $987,500 have been made on a contract of $1,750,000. The percentage of the TOTAL cost paid is

   A. 56.5   B. 57.2   C. 57.8   D. 58.2

7. Fire stopping PRIMARILY involves

   A. the placing of incombustible material over surfaces of combustible material
   B. replacing combustible with incombustible material
   C. the use of sprinklers and other protective devices
   D. the subdivision of large dead-air spaces

8. The MOST highly stressed rivet in in the gusset plate shown at the right is
   A. A
   B. B
   C. C
   D. D

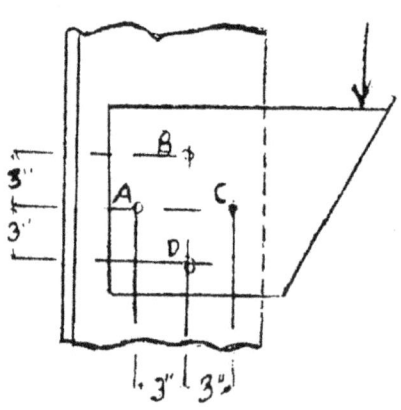

9. The built-in beam shown at the right will bend under load as shown in
   A. A
   B. B
   C. C
   D. D

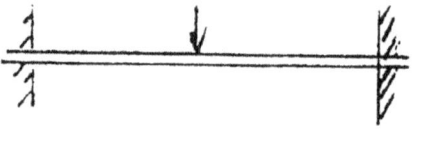

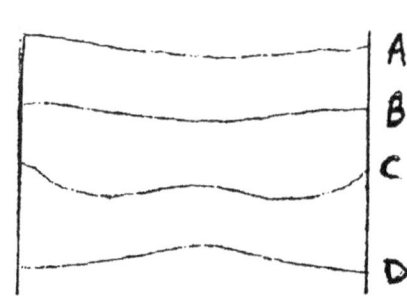

10. A vernier is a device used to
    A. measure fractional parts of a scale division
    B. measure the flow of water
    C. measure fluid pressure
    D. magnify objects

11. Of the following, the BEST pencil to use in taking field notes for a survey is
    A. H   B. 3H   C. 6H   D. 9H

12. A square is inscribed in a circle with a ten-inch diameter. The area of the square, in square inches, is
    A. 52   B. 51   C. 50   D. 49

13. A rectangular box is 10" long, 6" wide, and 4" high. The length of a diagonal drawn from the upper left rear corner to the lower right front corner is, in inches, MOST NEARLY
    A. 12.3   B. 12.4   C. 12.6   D. 12.8

14. A cam is USUALLY a _____ piece.
    A. circular, rotating   B. circular, non-rotating
    C. non-circular, rotating   D. non-circular, non-rotating

15. A right circular cone is 12 inches high, and the diameter of the base is 10 inches. The surface area of the cone is, in square inches, MOST NEARLY

   A. 196   B. 204   C. 210   D. 214

16. Of the following terms, the one which is LEAST related to the others is

   A. spindle   B. key   C. bolt   D. rivet

Questions 17-20.

DIRECTIONS: Each of Questions 17 through 20 is related to one of the lettered items below. Mark the letter of the related item in the space at the right.

17. Sub punch

   A. mortar joint   B. bridging
   C. roofing   D. ream

18. Flashing

   A. mortar joint   B. bridging
   C. roofing   D. ream

19. Joist

   A. mortar joint   B. bridging
   C. roofing   D. ream

20. Point

   A. mortar joint   B. bridging
   C. roofing   D. ream

21. Of the following terms, the one which is LEAST related to the others is

   A. bevel   B. pitch
   C. gage   D. edge distance

22. In differential leveling, the following shots were taken from a single set-up: on T.P.#1, 5.643; on T.P.#2, 8.159. T.P.#1 is _____ than T.P.#2 by _____.

   A. *higher;* 13.802   B. *lower;* 13.802
   C. *higher;* 2.516   D. *lower;* 2.516

23. Of the following terms, the one which is LEAST related to the others is

   A. course   B. stud   C. bat   D. bond

24.
A.

B.

C.

D.

In the symbols shown above, the one which represents a battery is

A. A   B. B   C. C   D. D

25. A 6" diameter steel pipe, 100 feet long, installed at 60° F conveys steam at 220° F. If the coefficient of linear expansion is 0.0000065 per degree Fahrenheit, the number of feet that the pipe expands is MOST NEARLY

A. .098   B. .104   C. .108   D. .116

KEY (CORRECT ANSWERS)

1.	B	11.	B
2.	C	12.	C
3.	A	13.	A
4.	D	14.	C
5.	D	15.	B
6.	A	16.	A
7.	D	17.	D
8.	C	18.	C
9.	B	19.	B
10.	A	20.	A

21. A
22. C
23. B
24. C
25. B

SOLUTIONS TO PROBLEMS

1. ANSWER: B
   Power = (3000)(6) = 18,000 ft-lb/sec.
   One HP = 550 ft-lb/sec.
   P = 18,000/550 = 32.7 HP

2. ANSWER: C
   Mechanical advantage = 2
   2F = 500; F = 250

3. ANSWER: A
   Wt. of water = 446 - 225 = 221
   Wt. of oil = 419 - 225 = 194
   Sp. gr. = 194/221 = 0.875

6. ANSWER: A

   $$\frac{9.875 \times 10^5}{1.75 \times 10^5} \times 10^2 = 56.5\%$$

12. ANSWER: C
    Diagonal of square = x/2

    Then $10 = x\sqrt{2}$

    $x = 10\sqrt{2}$

    Field of square = x^2

    $x^2 = (10/\sqrt{2})^2 = 100/2 = 50$

    <u>OR</u>

    A(field of square) = x^2 and
    $x^2 = 5^2 + 5^2 - 50$

    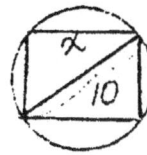

13. ANSWER: A
    $y^2 = 10^2 + 6^2 = 136"$
    $x^2 = y^2 + 4^2 = 152"$
    $x = \sqrt{152} = 12.33"$ (most nearly)

    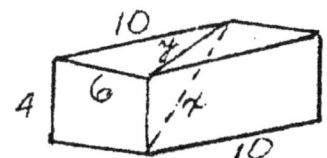

15. ANSWER: B

    The curved surface of a right circular cone is $\pi r\sqrt{r^2 + h^2}$

    A = $(\pi)(5)\sqrt{25+144} = 65\pi \sim 204$ (does not include area of the base)

22. ANSWER: C
    The larger number read on the scale refers to the lower level: 8.159 - 5.643 = 2.516

25. ANSWER: B
    Expansion = (100 ft.)(220 - 60°)(6.5 x 10⁻⁶) - 0.104 ft.

TEST 3

DIRECTIONS: Each question or incomplete statement is followed by several suggested answers or completions. Select the one that BEST answers the question or completes the statement. *PRINT THE LETTER OF THE CORRECT ANSWER IN THE SPACE AT THE RIGHT.*

1. Of the symbols shown above for materials in section, the one representing glass is

    A. A   B. B   C. C   D. D

    1._____

2. Of the symbols shown in the question above, for materials in section, the one representing cast iron is

    A. A   B. B   C. C   D. D

    2._____

Questions 3-6.

DIRECTIONS: Each of Questions 3 through 6 is related but in an opposite sense to one of the items marked A, B, C, and D. As an example, the terms *longitudinal* and *transverse* are related in that they both refer to direction, but, of course, the directions are at right angles. Indicate in the space at the right the OPPOSITE to the terms in these questions.

3. Tap

    A. Mantissa   B. Departure   C. Spiget   D. Die

    3._____

4. Bell

    A. Mantissa   B. Departure   C. Spiget   D. Die

    4._____

5. Latitude

    A. Mantissa   B. Departure   C. Spiget   D. Die

    5._____

6. Characteristic

    A. Mantissa   B. Departure   C. Spiget   D. Die

    6._____

Questions 7-11.

DIRECTIONS: In each of the following groups of drawings, the top view and front elevation of an object are shown at the left. At the right are four drawings, one of which represents the end elevation of the object as seen from the right. Select the drawing which represents the CORRECT end elevation.

    NOTE: The first group is shown as a sample only. Which drawing represents the CORRECT end elevation?

    A. A   B. B   C. C   D. D

2 (#3)

The CORRECT answer is C.

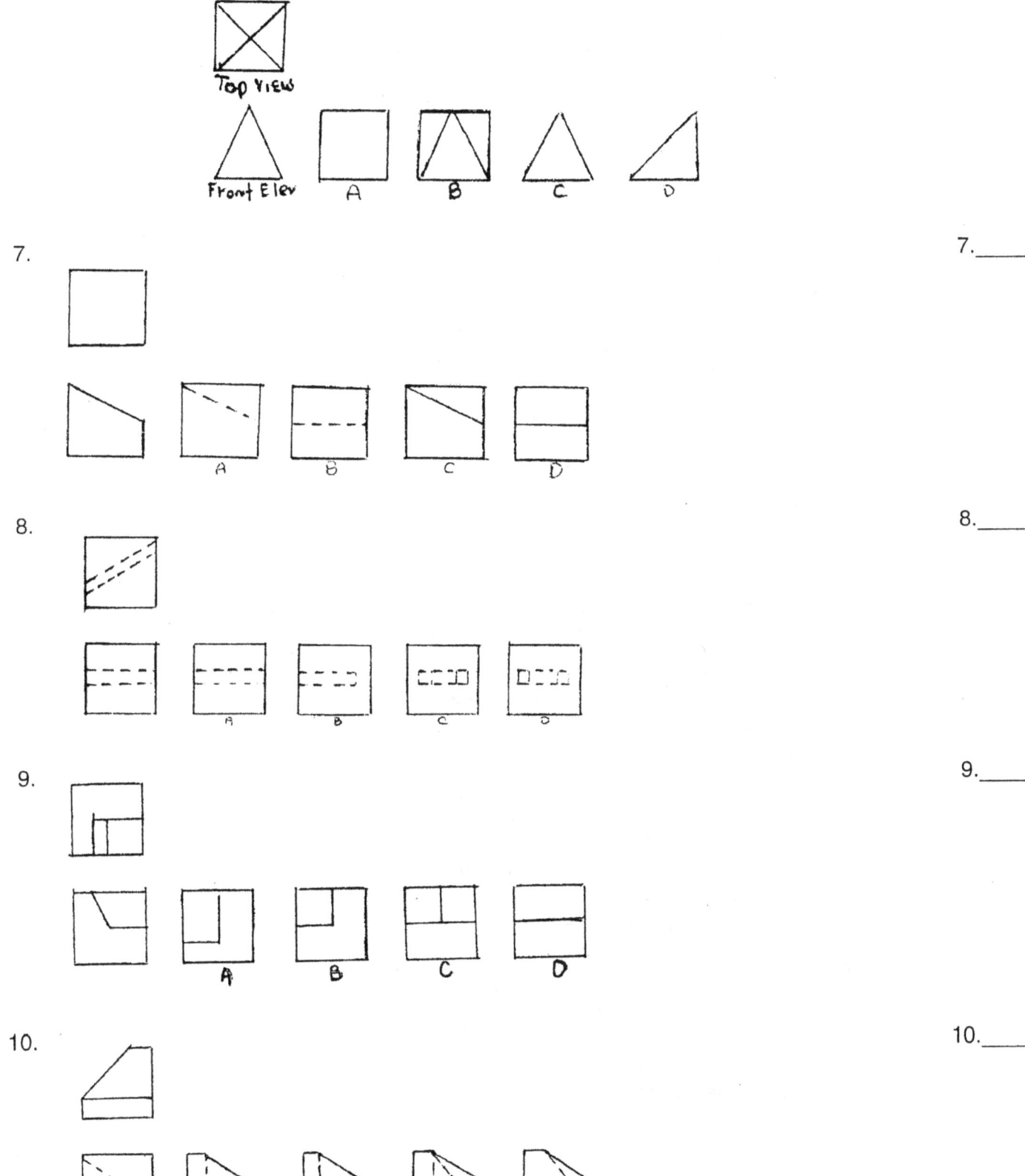

11.

[Figure: top view of square pyramid shape with options A, B, C, D showing different unfoldings/views]

11.____

12. Ten-penny nails

    A. are 10 inches long
    B. cost 10 cents per dozen
    C. weigh 10 pounds per thousand
    D. are not a commercial size

12.____

13. A dimension on a blueprint marked 3'4" is scaled and found to be 1 1/4". A second dimension on the same print scales 2 7/16".
The second dimension should be marked

    A. 6'3"   B. 6'6"   C. 6'8"   D. 6'9"

13.____

14. The logarithm of 2 is 0.30103. The logarithm of 0.25 is

    A. 9.39689-10
    B. 9.39791-10
    C. 9.39793-10
    D. 9.39796-10

14.____

15. A 1:2:3 1/2 concrete has a water-cement ratio of 6 gallons per sack of cement. The strength of the concrete can be increased by decreasing the

    A. ratio of the fine aggregate to cement
    B. ratio of the coarse aggregate to cement
    C. ratio of both fine and coarse aggregate to cement
    D. water-cement ratio

15.____

16. A spiral easement curve is NOT used

    A. to connect a tangent and a circular curve
    B. to connect two circular curves of different radii
    C. to connect two tangents
    D. at any time in highway work

16.____

17. Batter boards are used to

    A. define construction lines on the ground
    B. prevent splatter of concrete when pouring
    C. absorb shock in construction work
    D. barricade the construction area

17.____

18. In surveying, *double hubbing* or *double reversing* is done with a

    A. transit   B. level   C. tape   D. alidado

18.____

19. The inner surfaces of forms for concrete are oiled 19.____

   A. to prevent rusting
   B. to make removal of forms easier
   C. to prevent honeycombing
   D. when a stiff concrete mixture is being used

20. Installation of a sprinkler system would be LEAST complicated when the type of building construction is 20.____

   A. flat slab
   B. beam and girder
   C. steel frame
   D. brick bearing wall

21. Of the following items, the one which is NOT an opening protective is fire 21.____

   A. door B. tower C. shutter D. window

22. A load is to be supported by two 2 x 4's on a long simple span. 22.____
    The BEST way to arrange the 2 x 4's for maximum strength is

   A.

   B.

   C.

   D.

Questions 23-24.

   DIRECTIONS: Questions 23 and 24 are to be answered on the basis of the truss shown below.

23. The compression chord member is marked 23.____

   A. A B. B C. C D. D

24. The tension chord member is marked 24.____

   A. A B. B C. C D. D

25. A small by-pass on a large gate valve serves PRIMARILY 25.____

   A. to reduce the unbalanced pressure on the gate when opening the valve
   B. as a by-pass in case the valve cannot be opened
   C. to meter the flow through the valve
   D. to tell which way the water is flowing

KEY (CORRECT ANSWERS)

1.	B	11.	A
2.	D	12.	C
3.	D	13.	B
4.	C	14.	C
5.	B	15.	D
6.	A	16.	C
7.	D	17.	A
8.	C	18.	A
9.	B	19.	B
10.	A	20.	A

21. B
22. A
23. B
24. C
25. A

———

SOLUTIONS TO PROBLEMS

7. ANSWER: D
The perspective drawings are as follows:

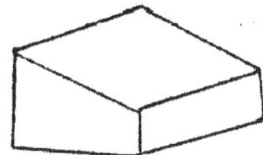

8. ANSWER: C

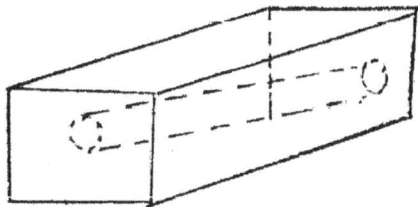

9. ANSWER: B

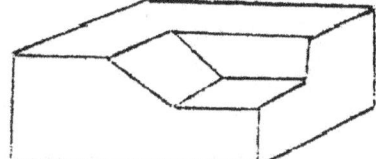

10. ANSWER: A

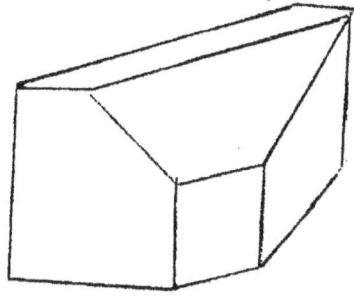

(As seen from rear of front elevation)

11. ANSWER: A

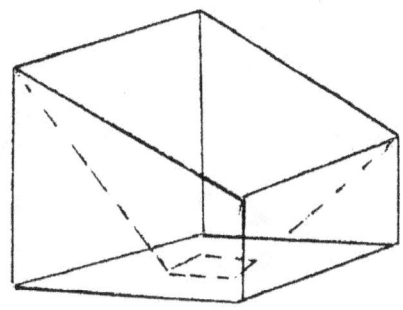

13. ANSWER: B
Scale = 5/4 in. per 40 in. = 1/32 in./in.
At a scale of 2 7/16 in., the second dimension is
(39/16)(32) = 78 in. = 6'6"

14. ANSWER: C
Log (1/4) = log 2^{-2} = (-2 x 0.30103) = 0.60206
= 9.39794-10

TEST 4

DIRECTIONS: Each question or incomplete statement is followed by several suggested answers or completions. Select the one that BEST answers the question or completes the statement. *PRINT THE LETTER OF THE CORRECT ANSWER IN THE SPACE AT THE RIGHT.*

1. The joints of bell-and-spigot cast iron water mains are filled with

    A. lead B. copper C. rubber D. oakum

2. Parallax exists in a transit when the

    A. line of sight is parallel to the long bubble
    B. cross-hairs appear to move over the object sighted when the observer's eye is moved slightly
    C. line of sight is perpendicular to the horizontal axis
    D. vertical axis is perpendicular to the horizontal axis

3. In unlined tunnel work, survey points are USUALLY located on

    A. the roof B. the walls
    C. the floor D. suspended platforms

4. The grit chamber of a sewage plant removes heavy solids such as sand by

    A. allowing the sewage to flow over a weir
    B. reducing the velocity of flow
    C. stopping the flow completely
    D. screens

5. Small sewer pipe is USUALLY made of

    A. cast iron, cement lined B. steel
    C. concrete D. vitrified clay

6. A timber weighing 500 pounds is to be dragged over a stone floor with a rope which makes an angle of 45 with the horizontal.
    If the coefficient of static friction is 0.4, the tension in the rope necessary to start the timber moving is, in pounds, MOST NEARLY

    A. 196 B. 202 C. 208 D. 214

7. A stadia survey would MOST probably be made in connection with

    A. a building layout
    B. a topographic map
    C. the location of bridge piers
    D. the erection of steel

8. The flanges and web of an H-section 12" wide by 12" deep are one inch thick. Steel weighs 490 pounds per cubic foot.
    A 10'0" length of this column would weigh, in pounds, MOST NEARLY

    A. 1150 B. 1250 C. 1350 D. 1450

9. The term *bond,* as used in connection with brick work, refers to the

   A. adhesion of mortar to brick
   B. metal anchors used to tie beams to wall
   C. arrangement of the bricks within the wall
   D. ties used to hold the brick to the backing

10.

   Loads: 10,000 at left; 20,000 at 8'0" from left; 20,000 at 12'0" further right.

   The center of gravity of the three concentrated loads shown in the sketch above is located a distance, in feet, from the right load of

   A. 8.4   B. 8.6   C. 8.8   D. 9.0

11. A Philadelphia Rod which can be used with or without a target

   A. is a sighting pole used for line work
   B. has a movable ribbon
   C. has a pointed shoe
   D. has graduations 0.01 feet wide

12. An airplane is flying at 240 mph (air speed). A wind of 100 mph is blowing at right angles to the longitudinal axis of the plane.
    The ground speed of the airplane is, in mph,

   A. 220   B. 240   C. 260   D. 280

Questions 13-17.

DIRECTIONS: Each of Questions 13 through 17 is related to one of the lettered items below. Indicate the CORRECT answer.

13. Fillet

   A. buck   B. cable   C. parapet
   D. bond   E. weld   F. plaster

14. Coping

   A. buck   B. cable   C. parapet
   D. bond   E. weld   F. plaster

15. Jamb

   A. buck   B. cable   C. parapet
   D. bond   E. weld   F. plaster

16. Stretcher

   A. buck   B. cable   C. parapet
   D. bond   E. weld   F. plaster

17. Bx

   A. buck   B. cable   C. parapet
   D. bond   E. weld   F. plaster

18. A block of wood of specific gravity 0.6 weighs 10 pounds. Its volume, in cubic feet, is MOST NEARLY

   A. .027   B. 0.27   C. 2.7   D. 27

19. A rectangular barge weighs 1,000,000 pounds when fully loaded and has outside dimensions of 60 feet long, 30 feet wide, and 10 feet deep.
   In fresh water, it sinks to a depth, in feet, MOST NEARLY of

   A. 7.7   B. 7.9   C. 8.9   D. 9.9

20. A gas in a compressor cylinder under an absolute pressure of 14.7 pounds per square inch has a volume of 6 cubic inches. It is compressed so slowly that its temperature does not vary, to a pressure of 100 pounds per square inch absolute.
   Its volume now is, in cubic inches, MOST NEARLY

   A. 0.58   B. 0.68   C. 0.78   D. 0.88

21. A quantity of mercury is heated, and Fahrenheit and Centigrade thermometers are immersed in it. The reading on the Fahrenheit scale is exactly twice the reading on the centigrade scale.
   The reading on the Fahrenheit scale is

   A. 320   B. 360   C. 400   D. 440

22. A piece of metal 6 inches in diameter is being turned in a lathe.
   If the recommended cutting speed is 500 feet per minute, the required revolutions per minute of the spindle is MOST NEARLY

   A. 320   B. 2130   C. 1320   D. 120

23. A building is being raised by a jack preparatory to underpinning the structure. The load on the jack is 4000 pounds. The jack screw has a pitch of 2 threads per inch.
   Ignoring friction, the force, in pounds, applied at a point on a capstan bar 3'0" from the axis of the jack screw required to raise the building is MOST NEARLY

   A. 288   B. 144   C. 72   D. 9

24. Of the following items, the one that is LEAST related to the others in function is

   A. bulldozer   B. clamshell
   C. backhoe   D. A-frame

25. One pound of lead at 200° F is placed in one pound of water which is at a temperature of 60° F. In a short time, both attain the same temperature of 64.3.
   The specific heat of lead as determined above, in BTU per pound per degree Fahrenheit, is MOST NEARLY

   A. .0137   B. .0217   C. .0317   D. .0537

KEY (CORRECT ANSWERS)

1.	A	11.	D
2.	B	12.	C
3.	A	13.	E
4.	B	14.	C
5.	D	15.	A
6.	B	16.	D
7.	B	17.	B
8.	A	18.	B
9.	C	19.	C
10.	C	20.	D

21. A
22. A
23. D
24. D
25. C

———

SOLUTIONS TO PROBLEMS

6. ANSWER: B
   F = kN, where N = normal force between the surfaces, and
   k = coefficient of static friction
   ∴ F min. = (500)(0.4) = 200

   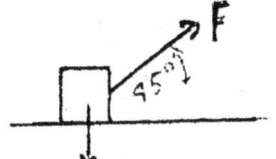

8. ANSWER: A
   Two sections have volume,
   V_1 = (10)(1)(1/12).
   One section has V_2 = (10/12)(1/12)(10)
   Weight = $(2V_1 + V_2)$(490) ~ 1150

   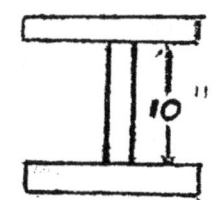

10. ANSWER: C
    50,000x = (20,000)(12)+(10,000)(20)   x = 8.8

    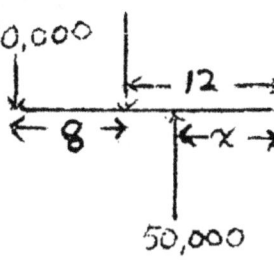

12. ANSWER: C
    $V = \sqrt{100^2 + 200^2} = 260$

    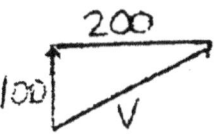

18. ANSWER: B
    Density = (0.6)(62.4) lb./ft.^{3}
    Volume = 10/(0.6)(62.4) ~ 0.27

19. ANSWER: C
    10^6 lbs. will displace 106/62.4 = 1.6 x 10^4 ft.^{3} of water.
    Since cross section = 60 x 30 ft.^{2}, depth = 1.6 x 10^4/60 x30 = 8.9 ft.

20. ANSWER: D
    Boyle's law: PV = constant
    (14.7)(6)   = (100 x V)
            V = 0.882 ft.^{3}

21. ANSWER: A
    In general, °F. = (9/5)° C + 32
    When F = 2C,
    ∴   F = (9/5)(F/2) + 32
        F = 320°

22. ANSWER: A

The initial circumference of the piece is $\pi D = \pi/2$ ft.

$\therefore 500/(\pi/2) = 320$ ft. per min.

23. ANSWER: D

The mechanical advantage of a screw or jack =

$2\pi l/p$ (l = length of force arm, p = pitch of the screw)

Mech. Adv. = $(2\pi)(36)/0.5 = 144\pi$.

Force = $4000/144\pi \sim 9$ lb.

24. ANSWER: C

$Q = m C_p \Delta t$

For water, $C_p = 1$ Btu/lb./°F.
$(1.0)(1.0)(64.3 - 60) = (1.0)(C_p)(200 - 64.3)$
$C_p = 4.3/135.7 = 0.0317$

EXAMINATION SECTION
TEST 1

DIRECTIONS: Each question or incomplete statement is followed by several suggested answers or completions. Select the one that BEST answers the question or completes the statement. *PRINT THE LETTER OF THE CORRECT ANSWER IN THE SPACE AT THE RIGHT.*

1. The ultimate strength of a short 16" x 16" concrete column with 8 #8 steel bars with f_c = 4000 psi and f_y = 69000 psi is, in kips, MOST NEARLY
    A. 1290   B. 1320   C. 1350   D. 1380

2. Transverse ties with the vertical steel #10 bars or smaller have a minimum size of _____ bar.
    A. #2   B. #3   C. #4   D. #5

3. The capacity reduction, ϕ, for shear on a concrete beam section is
    A. .75   B. .80   C. .85   D. .90

4. The balanced steel ratio occurs when the steel
    A. and concrete fail simultaneously   B. fails before the concrete
    C. fails after the concrete   D. reaches its ultimate strength

5. The minimum requirement of $p = \frac{200}{fy}$ is necessary in concrete beam design to insure that the
    A. concrete will not fail before the reinforcing steel
    B. member does not lose strength when it first cracks
    C. bonding between steel and concrete does not fail
    D. deflection of the beam is not excessive

6. In ultimate strength design, the ϕ value for flexure without axial load is the largest of all ϕ factors because
    A. the loads are less variable in bending than they are for axial loads
    B. there is more variability in shear loads than in bending moments
    C. steel has a greater coefficient of expansion than concrete
    D. there is less variability in steel strength than in concrete strength

7. If, in the design of a reinforced concrete beam section, the service moment is 40 k-ft. for dead load and 90 k-ft. for live load, the load factored moment is, in kip feet, MOST NEARLY (ϕ is not included)
    A. 190   B. 209   C. 219   D. 229

2 (#1)

Questions 8-12.

DIRECTIONS: Questions 8 through 12, inclusive, refer to the reinforced concrete beam section shown below.

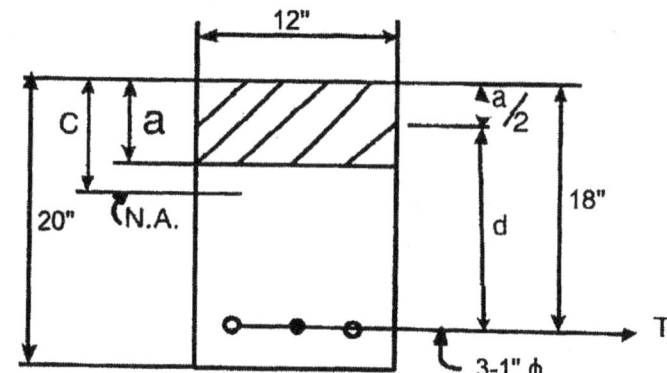

$f_c = 4000 \#/\square'$

$f_y = 60,000 \#/\square''$

Area of 1" ϕ = .79 $\square''$

8. The proportion of steel to concrete, p, is MOST NEARLY
   A. .011   B. .010   C. .009   D. .008

9. The maximum value of T, in kips, is MOST NEARLY
   A. 138   B. 142   C. 146   D. 150

10. The value of *a* corresponding to the maximum value of T is, in inches, MOST NEARLY
    A. 3.5   B. 3.8   C. 4.2   D. 4.6

11. The moment, in foot kips, that the beam section can carry, assuming $\phi = 0.9$, is, in foot kips, MOST NEARLY
    A. 173   B. 178   C. 183   D. 188

12. The value of *c* is, in inches, MOST NEARLY
    A. 3.7   B. 3.9   C. 4.1   D. 4.3

13. Granite is the type of rock that is
    A. silicious
    B. igneous
    C. sedimentary
    D. metamorphic

14. In a trial batch of concrete, the fine aggregate has a weight of 148 pounds. It has 6% of its weight in water. The specific gravity of the fine aggregate is 2.65.
    The absolute volume of the fine aggregate, in cubic feet, is MOST NEARLY
    A. .84   B. .82   C. .80   D. .78

15. The optimum concrete mix for a given structural element having a given water-cement ratio would have a
    A. maximum allowable size of coarse aggregate and a minimum allowable slump
    B. minimum allowable size of coarse aggregate and a minimum amount of slump

C. maximum allowable size of coarse aggregate and a maximum allowable slump
D. minimum size of coarse aggregate and a maximum slump

16. Bulking of sand
    A. varies inversely with the water content
    B. is greater with coarse sand than with fine sand
    C. decreases when there is high moisture in the atmosphere
    D. is a maximum when the water content is about 6% by weight

17. A medium-curing cutback asphalt would MOST likely contain as a solvent
    A. gasoline
    B. naphtha
    C. an oil of low volatility
    D. kerosene

18. The PRIMARY reason for using cutback asphalt is that it
    A. gives a harder riding surface
    B. is more resistant to softening at high outdoor temperatures
    C. requires little or no heat during placing
    D. does not age as rapidly as ordinary asphalt

19. Emulsified asphalt is an emulsion primarily of asphalt and
    A. toluene   B. water   C. kerosene   D. naphtha

Questions 20-22.

DIRECTIONS: Questions 20 through 22 are to be answered on the basis of the 400' vertical curve shown below.

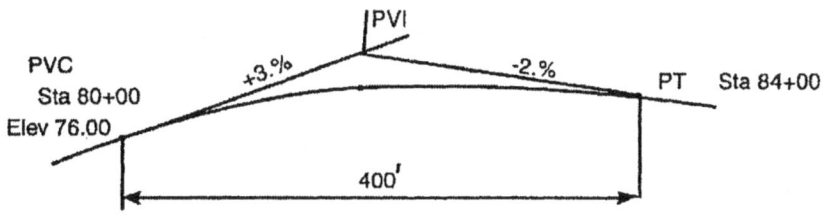

20. The elevation of the vertical curve at Sta 82+00 is, in feet, MOST NEARLY
    A. 79.25   B. 79.50   C. 79.75   D. 80.00

21. The station at the high point of the vertical curve is MOST NEARLY
    A. 82+20   B. 82+40   C. 82+60   D. 82+80

22. The elevation of the high point of the vertical curve is, in feet, MOST NEARLY
    A. 79.60   B. 79.70   C. 79.80   D. 79.90

23. If a 1° central angle of a circle intercepts an arc of 100', the radius of the circle is, in feet, MOST NEARLY
    A. 5709   B. 5729   C. 5749   5769

24. A circular horizontal curve has a radius of 1600' and a tangent length of 950'. The length of the curve from PC to PT is, in feet, MOST NEARLY
   A. 1714.6   B. 1724.6   C. 1734.6   D. 1744.6

25.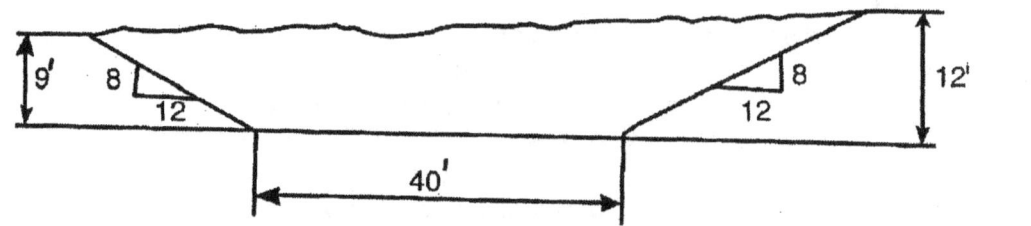

The cross-section of an area in cut in a highway excavation is shown above. the area of the cut is, in square feet, MOST NEARLY
   A. 562   B. 582   C. 602   D. 622

KEY (CORRECT ANSWERS)

1.	B	11.	A
2.	B	12.	C
3.	C	13.	B
4.	A	14.	A
5.	B	15.	A
6.	D	16.	D
7.	B	17.	D
8.	A	18.	C
9.	B	19.	B
10.	A	20.	B

21.	B
22.	A
23.	B
24.	A
25.	A

TEST 2

DIRECTIONS: Each question or incomplete statement is followed by several suggested answers or completions. Select the one that BEST answers the question or completes the statement. *PRINT THE LETTER OF THE CORRECT ANSWER IN THE SPACE AT THE RIGHT.*

1. The water pressure in the pipe as shown by the manometer at the right is, in pounds per square inch, MOST NEARLY
   A. 5.5
   B. 5.9
   C. 6.3
   D. 6.7

   1._____

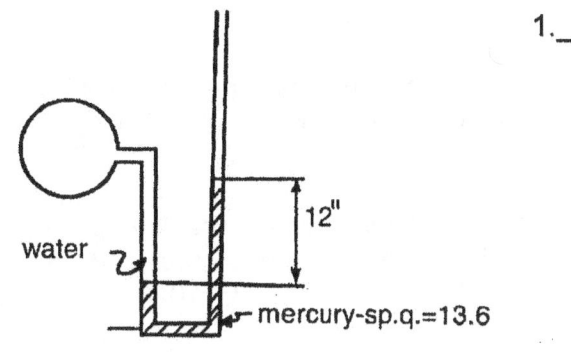

2. The theoretical discharge over a rectangular weir of length L is $Q = cL\sqrt{2qHx}$, where x is
   A. ½   B. 1   C. 3/2   D. 2

   2._____

3. If one cubic foot of water per second under a head of 80' is delivered to a turbine, the horsepower that the turbine can deliver, assuming no losses, is
   A. 5   B. 7   C. 9   D. 11

   3._____

Questions 4-5.

DIRECTIONS: Questions 4 and 5 are to be answered on the basis of the diagram below of the 3" outlet from a tank of water.

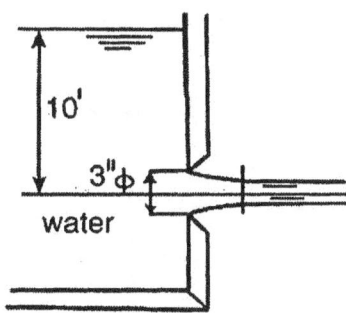

4. The velocity of the water at the point of discharge is, in feet per second, MOST NEARLY
   A. 22   B. 25   C. 28   D. 30

   4._____

5. The discharge rate, in cubic feet per second, is MOST NEARLY
   A. .50   B. .75   C. 1.00   D. 1.25

   5._____

6. When a sewer is built using vitrified clay pipe, construction starts from the _____ elevation with the bell facing _____.
   A. highest; downward
   B. highest; upward
   C. lowest; downward
   D. lowest; upward

7. A sewer that runs along a waterfront and carries sewage into a sewage treatment plant is known as a(n) _____ sewer.
   A. outfall   B. intercepting   C. relief   D. combined

8. The change in temperature, in degrees Fahrenheit, that will cause a 100 foot steel tape to lengthen .01 feet is MOST NEARLY
   A. 5   B. 10   C. 15   D. 20

9. A map is drawn to a scale of 1 inch equals 200 feet. Contours are drawn at intervals of 2 feet.
   If the distance between two adjacent contours measures ½ inch, the slope of the surface is MOST NEARLY
   A. 2%   B. 3%   C. 4%   D. 5%

10. The angle φ at E caused by a moment M at E is
    A. $\dfrac{ML}{EI}$
    B. $\dfrac{ML}{2EI}$
    C. $\dfrac{ML}{3EI}$
    D. $\dfrac{ML}{4EI}$

Questions 11-12.

DIRECTIONS: Questions 11 and 12 are to be answered on the basis of the following diagram.

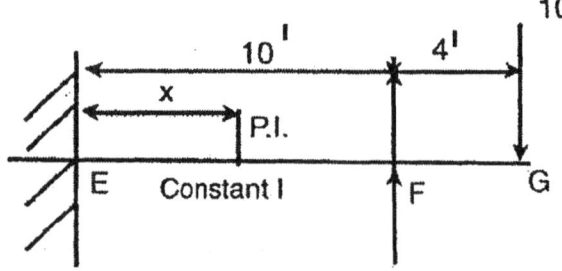

11. The magnitude of the moment at E is MOST NEARLY
    A. 20^{lk} B. 23^{lk} C. 27^{lk} D. 30^{lk}

12. The vertical reaction at E is, in kips, MOST NEARLY _____ downward.
    A. 6^K B. 5^K C. 4^K D. 3^K

3 (#2)

13. The distance x from the point E to the point of inflection is, in feet, MOST NEARLY 13.____
    A. 4.33   B. 4.00   C. 3.67   D. 3.33

Questions 14-15.

DIRECTIONS: Questions 14 and 15 are to be answered on the basis of the cantilever beam shown below.

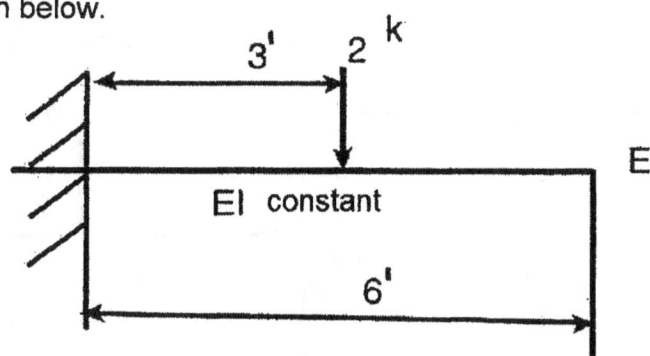

14. The deflection at the end E of the cantilever beam shown above is 14.____
    A. $30^{k13/EI}$ B. $34^{k13/EI}$ C. $40^{k13/EI}$ D. $45^{k13/EI}$

15. The slope of the beam at E is 15.____
    A. $6^{k12/EI}$ B. $9^{k12/EI}$ C. $12^{k12/EI}$ D. $15^{k12/EI}$

16. With both ends of the beam EF fixed, the magnitude of the fixed end moment at E is, in foot-kips, 16.____
    A. 18
    B. 21
    C. 24
    D. 270

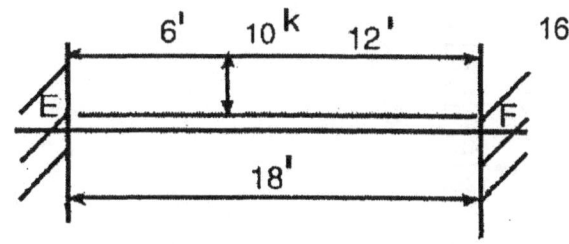

17. The conjugate beam for the beam shown at the right would be 17.____

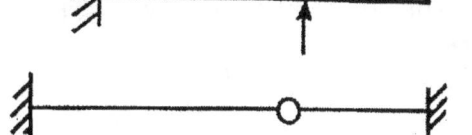

A.

B.

C.

D.

18. The deflection at the center of the beam shown at the right is
    A. $\dfrac{PL^3}{16EI}$
    B. $\dfrac{PL^3}{32EI}$
    C. $\dfrac{PL^3}{48EI}$
    D. $\dfrac{PL^3}{64EI}$

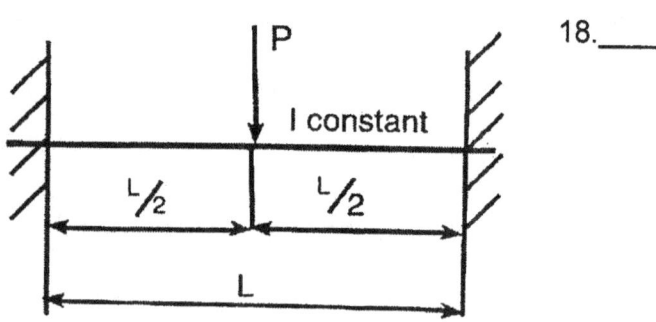

18.____

19. The deflection at the center of the beam shown at the right is
    A. $\dfrac{PL^3}{48EI}$
    B. $\dfrac{PL^3}{96EI}$
    C. $\dfrac{PL^3}{192EI}$
    D. $\dfrac{PL^3}{184EI}$

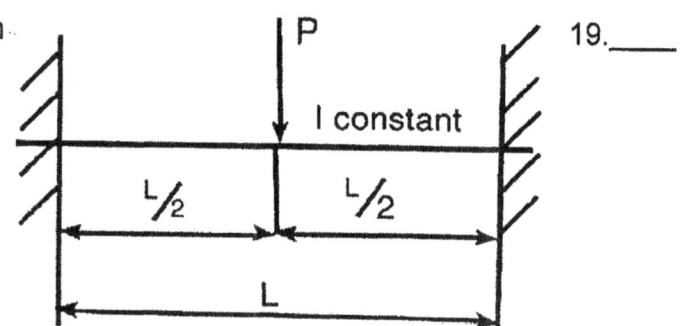

19.____

20. The offset deflection on the fixed end beam in terms of L, M, E, and I is
    A. $\dfrac{ML^2}{6EI}$
    B. $\dfrac{ML^2}{8EI}$
    C. $\dfrac{ML^2}{10EI}$
    D. $\dfrac{ML^2}{12EI}$

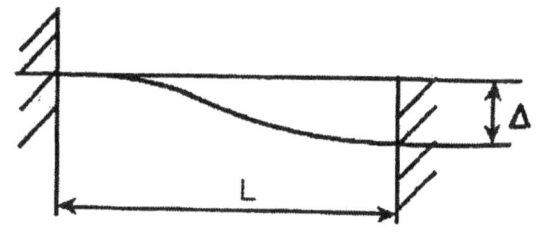

20.____

21. If the deflection on a beam is $\dfrac{KPL^3}{EI}$, where K is dimensionless, L is in feet, P is in kips, E is in kips per square inch, and I is in inches^4, the constant that the resulting product must be multiplied by in order to have the deflection in inches is
    A. 12   B. 12^2 C. 12^3 D. 12^4

21.____

22. The maximum moment on the beam shown at the right, in foot-kips, is
    A. 16.5
    B. 18.5
    C. 20.5
    D. 22.5

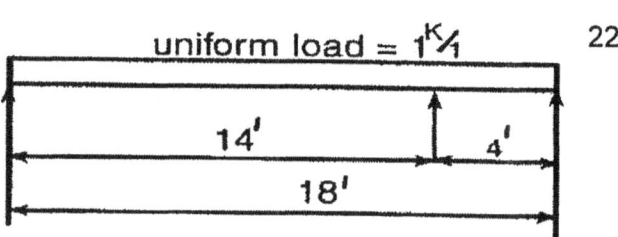

22.____

Questions 23-24.

DIRECTIONS: Questions 23 and 24 are to be answered on the basis of the beam EF shown below with a triangular loading.

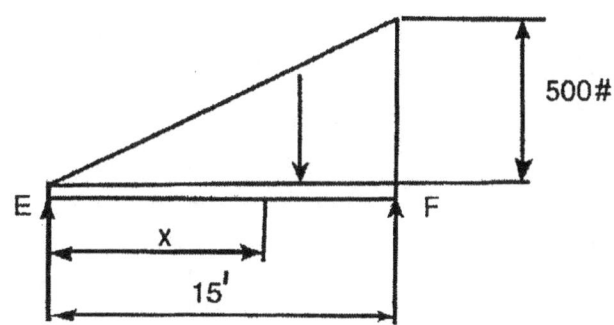

23. The distance x to the point of shears is, in feet, MOST NEARLY 23.____
    A. 8.00   B. 8.33   C. 8.66   D. 9.00

24. The maximum moment on the beam is, in foot-kips, MOST NEARLY 24.____
    A. 6.82   B. 7.22   C. 7.62   D. 8.03

25. The change in length of member EF due to the 10000 pound loads is, in inches, MOST NEARLY 25.____
    A. .032
    B. .043
    C. .056
    D. .067

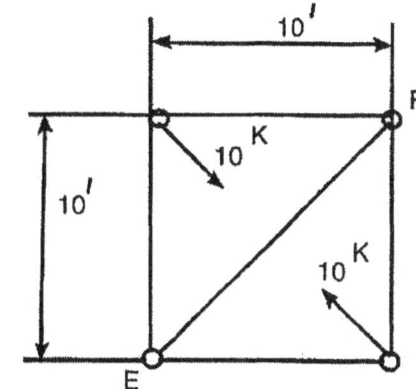

$E = 30,000 K/\square"$
Cross-section area of EF = 1 square inch

KEY (CORRECT ANSWERS)

1.	A	11.	A
2.	C	12.	A
3.	C	13.	D
4.	B	14.	D
5.	B	15.	B
6.	D	16.	D
7.	B	17.	D
8.	C	18.	C
9.	A	19.	C
10.	C	20.	A

21.	C
22.	C
23.	C
24.	B
25.	C

TEST 3

DIRECTIONS: Each question or incomplete statement is followed by several suggested answers or completions. Select the one that BEST answers the question or completes the statement. *PRINT THE LETTER OF THE CORRECT ANSWER IN THE SPACE AT THE RIGHT.*

Questions 1-5.

DIRECTIONS: Questions 1 through 5, inclusive, are to be answered on the basis of the bent with rigid connections at E, F, G, and H.

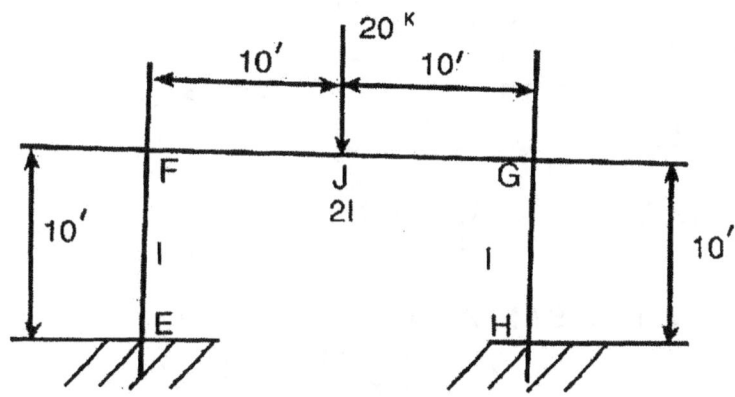

1. The vertical reaction at E is, in kips, MOST NEARLY 1.____
   A. 5   B. 7.5   C. 10   D. 12.5

2. The magnitude of the moment at F on beam FG is, in foot-kips, MOST NEARLY 2.____
   A. 25   B. 27.5   C. 30   D. 35

3. The magnitude of the moment at E on beam EF is, in foot-kips, MOST NEARLY 3.____
   A. 12.5   B. 13.8   C. 15   D. 17.5

4. The horizontal reaction at E is, in kips, MOST NEARLY 4.____
   A. 2.6   B. 3.0   C. 3.4   D. 3.8

5. The moment, in foot-kips, at J is 5.____
   A. 65   B. 70   C. 75   D. 80

Questions 6-11.

DIRECTIONS: Questions 6 through 11, inclusive, are to be answered on the basis of the following truss.

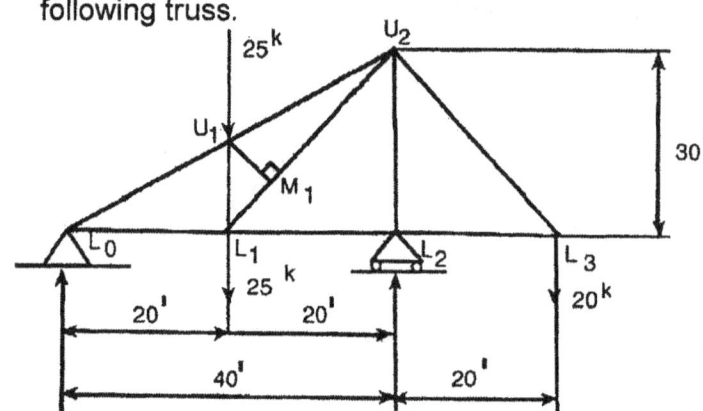

6. The length of the member U_1-M_1 is MOST NEARLY
   A. 8.3 ft.   B. 8.6 ft.   C. 8.9 ft.   D. 9.2 ft.

7. The load in member U_1-M_1 is MOST NEARLY
   A. 0
   B. 15k compression
   C. 20k compression
   D. 25k compression

8. The load in member U_2-L_2 is MOST NEARLY _____ compression.
   A. 55^k B. 50^k C. 45^k D. 40^k

9. The load in member U_1-L_1 is MOST NEARLY _____ compression.
   A. 10^k B. 15^k C. 20^k D. 25^k

10. The load in member L_1-U_2 is MOST NEARLY _____ tension.
    A. 50k   B. 55k   C. 60k   D. 65k

11. The load in member U_1-U_2 is MOST NEARLY _____ compression.
    A. 20k   B. 25k   C. 30k   D. 35k

12. If the center support of the uniformly loaded beam settles slightly, then the
    A. reaction at F increases
    B. magnitude of the moment at F increases
    C. magnitude of the shear at G decreases
    D. reaction at E increases

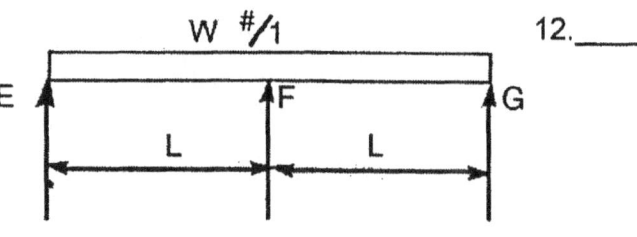

Questions 13-16.

DIRECTIONS: Questions 13 through 16, inclusive, are to be answered on the basis of the truss shown below carrying a uniform moving live load of 2 kips per foot.

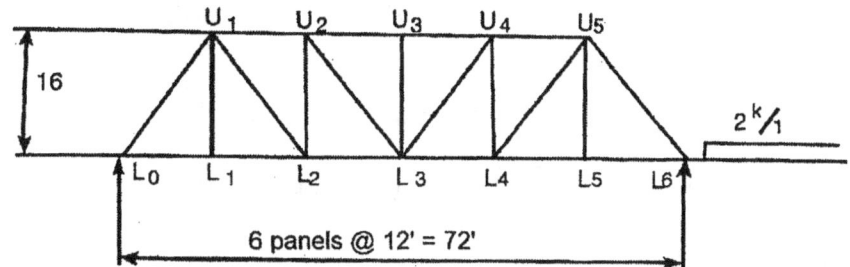

13. The type of truss shown above is known as a _____ truss.   13.____
    A. Pratt   B. Howe   C. Warren   D. Whipple

14. The influence line diagram for member U_2-L_3 is as shown in   14.____
    A. 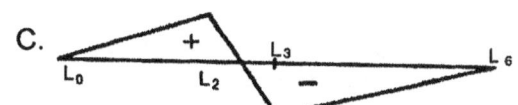   B.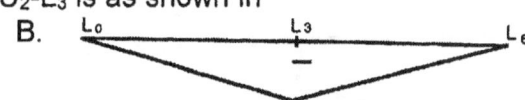
    C. 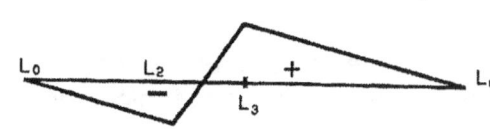   D.

15. The ordinate on the influence line diagram for U_2-L_3 at L_3 is MOST NEARLY   15.____
    A. 3/8   B. ½   C. 5/8   D. ¾

16. The maximum tensile load on U_2-L_3 caused by a $2^{k/1}$ live load coming from the right end of the truss is, in kips, MOST NEARLY   16.____
    A. 21   B. 23   C. 25   D. 27

17. The largest size weld that can be made in one pass is, in inches,   17.____
    A. 3/16   B. ¼   C. 5/16   D. 3/8

18. The maximum allowable shearing stress on fillet welds made with E7018 welding rods is _____ kips/sq.in.   18.____
    A. 18   B. 19   C. 20   D. 21

19. The symbol for field welding is as shown in   19.____
    A.    B.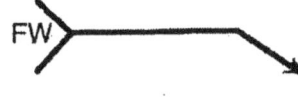
    C.   D.

20. A 3x3/8 plate is to be welded to the back of a channel to develop the full strength of the plate in tension. The allowable tensile stress in the plate is 24 k/▫". The allowable shearing stress in the ¼ weld is 21k/▫". The minimum length of weld needed is, in inches, MOST NEARLY
   A. 7½   B. 9   C. 10½   D. 12

21. The minimum size fillet weld to use on a ⁷⁄₈" thick plate is, in inches,
   A. ³⁄₁₆   B. ¼   C. ⁵⁄₁₆   D. ⅜

22. Shown below is a 5x5x½L to be welded to the gusset plate under the angle to carry a 60k load.

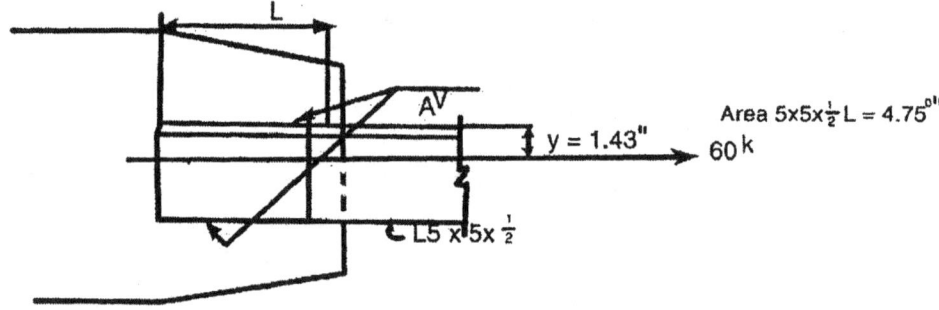

The allowable shear stress in the weld is 21k/▫". The center of gravity of the welds are to coincide with the center of gravity of L5x5x½. The length L is, in inches, MOST NEARLY
   A. 10.0   B. 11.5   C. 13.0   D. 14.5

23. Some of the bolts in a structural steel structure have square heads. The ASTM designation of these bolts would MOST likely be
   A. A307   B. A325   C. A490   D. A502

24. For high strength bolts in bearing, if Fu is the tensile strength of the steel connected by the bolts, with adequate bolts spacing, the allowable bearing stress is _____ Fu.
   A. 1.0   B. 1.25   C. 1.5   D. 1.75

25. The $\frac{d}{dx}(e^{\log x})$ is equal to
   A. e^x B. 1   C. $x \log x$ D. $\frac{1}{x}$

KEY (CORRECT ANSWERS)

1.	C	11.	B
2.	A	12.	D
3.	A	13.	A
4.	D	14.	D
5.	C	15.	C
6.	A	16.	D
7.	A	17.	C
8.	A	18.	D
9.	D	19.	D
10.	C	20.	A

21.	C
22.	B
23.	A
24.	C
25.	B

TEST 4

DIRECTIONS: Each question or incomplete statement is followed by several suggested answers or completions. Select the one that BEST answers the question or completes the statement. *PRINT THE LETTER OF THE CORRECT ANSWER IN THE SPACE AT THE RIGHT.*

Questions 1-2.

DIRECTIONS: Questions 1 and 2 are to be answered on the basis of the bolted connection supporting a 15k eccentric load shown below.

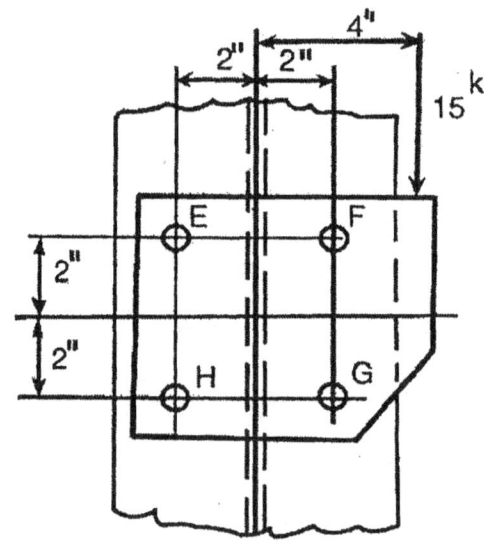

1. The bolts that carry the largest load are
   A. E and F B. F and G C. G and H D. H and E

2. The maximum load on a bolt is, in kips, MOST NEARLY
   A. 7.2 B. 7.6 C. 8.0 D. 8.4

3. The value of the determinant $\begin{vmatrix} 2 & 1 & 3 \\ 1 & 5 & -6 \\ 1 & 2 & 0 \end{vmatrix}$ is
   A. +3 B. +6 C. +9 D. +12

4. $\int_0^{\pi/4} \cos x \sin^2 x \, dx$ is equal to
   A. $\frac{\sqrt{2}}{10}$ B. $\frac{\sqrt{2}}{12}$ C. $\frac{\sqrt{2}}{14}$ D. $\frac{\sqrt{2}}{16}$

5. In the xy plane, the distance from point E to the line y = x + 2 is
   A. $\sqrt{2}$
   B. $2\sqrt{2}$
   C. $3\sqrt{3}$
   D. $4\sqrt{2}$

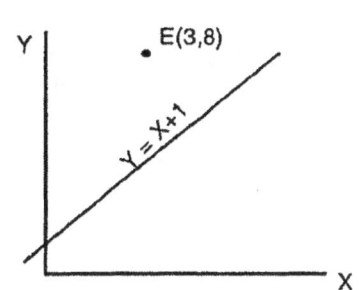

6. The area of the ellipse is $\frac{x^2}{a^2} + \frac{y^2}{b^2} = 1$
   A. $\frac{\pi ab}{4}$
   B. $\frac{\pi ab}{2}$
   C. πab
   D. $\frac{3}{2}\pi ab$

7. Of the following matrix multiplications, the one that cannot be carried out is
   A. $\begin{bmatrix} e & f \\ g & h \end{bmatrix} \begin{bmatrix} j \\ k \end{bmatrix}$
   B. $\begin{bmatrix} e & f \\ g & h \end{bmatrix} [j \; k]$
   C. $[e \; f \; g] \begin{bmatrix} h \\ j \\ k \end{bmatrix}$
   D. $\begin{bmatrix} e \\ f \\ g \end{bmatrix} [h \; j \; k]$

8. Of the following statements relating to matrix operations, the one that is NOT correct is the _____ law of _____ applies to matrices.
   A. associative; addition
   B. associative; multiplication
   C. commutative; addition
   D. commutative; multiplication

9. The volume of revolution formed by rotating the curve y = sin x about the x axis from x = 0 to x = π is
   A. π^2
   B. $\frac{x^2}{2}$
   C. $\frac{x^2}{3}$
   D. $\frac{x^2}{4}$

10. Based on the prismoidal formula, the volume of earth excavated in cubic yards, if one end is 6'x6', and the other end is 12'x12' and the length is 160', is MOST NEARLY
    A. 460
    B. 480
    C. 500
    D. 520

11. The sin(arc tan $\frac{1}{\sqrt{3}}$) is equal to
    A. $\frac{2}{\sqrt{2}}$
    B. $\frac{1}{2}$
    C. $\frac{\sqrt{3}}{2}$
    D. $\frac{\sqrt{3}}{3}$

12. The sum of the interior angles of an octagon is, in degrees, MOST NEARLY
    A. 960
    B. 1020
    C. 1080
    D. 1140

13. The modulus of elasticity of steel in the metric system is _____ x 10^6kPa.
    A. 210
    B. 240
    C. 270
    D. 300

14. If the density of aluminum is 173 #/cu.ft., the density of aluminum in the metric system is, in kg/m³,
    A. 2500
    B. 2590
    C. 2680
    D. 2770

15. One pound per square inch is equal to, in newtons per square meter, 15.____
    A. 5778   B. 6180   C. 6582   D. 6984

16. The moment at E on the beam shown at the right is, in foot-kips, MOST NEARLY 16.____
    A. 28
    B. 32
    C. 36
    D. 40

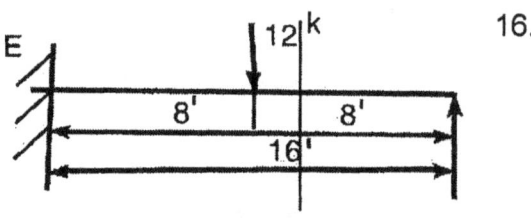

Questions 17-19.

DIRECTIONS: Questions 17 through 19 are to be answered on the basis of the simply supported beam shown below.

A wood beam 8x20# carries a uniform load (including the weight of the wood beam) of 800 #/1 including a 800# load 4 feet from the left end of a simply supported beam on a span of 16 feet as shown below.

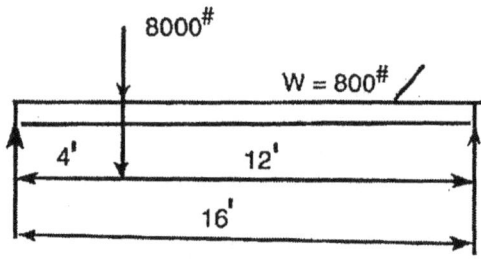 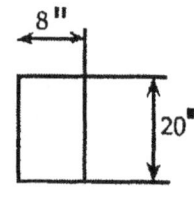

17. The of 0 shear is at a distance from the left support, in feet, MOST NEARLY 17.____
    A. 4.0   B. 4.5   C. 5.0   D. 5.5

18. The maximum bending stress is, in pounds per square inch, MOST NEARLY 18.____
    A. 900   B. 930   C. 960   D. 990

19. The maximum shearing stress is, in pounds per square inch, MOST NEARLY 19.____
    A. 116   B. 130   C. 146   D. 162

20. The cross-section area of a w 12x22 steel beam is, in square inches, MOST NEARLY 20.____
    A. 6.17   B. 6.47   C. 6.77   D. 7.07

21. A welding electrode is specified as E7018. 21.____
    Of the following statements relating to the electrode, the one that is CORRECT is the
    A. 70 relates to the tensile strength of the weld in kips per square inch
    B. 70 is the Charpy V-Notch Test requirement that must be met
    C. 1 represents the coating characteristic
    D. 8 represents the position code

22. In tall steel frame buildings, the columns are usually erected in lengths of _____ story(ies).
    A. 1   B. 2   C. 3   D. 4

23. In a L6x4x½, the distance from the back of the 4 inch leg to the center of gravity of the angle is, in inches, MOST NEARLY
    A. 1.60   B. 1.80   C. 2.00   D. 2.20

24. In the Atterberg Test for soil, a standard brass cup is partly filled with wet soil. A groove of standard dimension is cut in the soil. The cup is lifted and dropped one centimeter 25 times.
    The purpose of this test is to determine the _____ of the soil.
    A. plastic limit
    B. plastic index
    C. shrinkage limit
    D. liquid limit

25. In the Atterberg Test for soil, the water content at which a $1/8$ inch diameter thread of soil begins to crumble when rolled under the palm of the hand is known as the _____ of the soil.
    A. plastic limit
    B. plastic index
    C. shrinkage limit
    D. liquid limit

KEY (CORRECT ANSWERS)

1. B		11. B	
2. D		12. C	
3. C		13. A	
4. B		14. D	
5. B		15. D	
6. C		16. C	
7. B		17. D	
8. D		18. D	
9. B		19. A	
10. C		20. B	

21. A
22. B
23. C
24. D
25. A

EXAMINATION SECTION
TEST 1

DIRECTIONS: Each question or incomplete statement is followed by several suggested answers or completions. Select the one that BEST answers the question or completes the statement. *PRINT THE LETTER OF THE CORRECT ANSWER IN THE SPACE AT THE RIGHT.*

1. If $x = 3$ and $3x^4 - x + 4x^0 - 3x^{-1} = y$, then y equals 1._____
   A. 81 B. 235 C. 240 D. 243

2. If $\sqrt{x^2+9} - x = 1$, then x is 2._____
   A. 9 B. 5 C. 4 D. 2

3. If $1/x = y + 1/z$, then x is equal to 3._____
   A. $\dfrac{z+1}{yz+1}$ B. $\dfrac{y^2}{z}$ C. y^2 D. $\dfrac{z}{yz+1}$

4. The secant of $30°$ is 4._____
   A. $\dfrac{2}{\sqrt{3}}$ B. $\dfrac{\sqrt{3}}{2}$ C. $\dfrac{1}{\sqrt{2}}$ D. $\dfrac{-\sqrt{2}}{\sqrt{3}}$

5. If $\sqrt{x} = \dfrac{y^2}{z}$, then y is equal to 5._____
   A. $x^2 y^2$ B. $xz^{\frac{3}{2}}$ C. $(x^2 z)^{\frac{1}{3}}$ D. $(xz^2)^{\frac{1}{4}}$

6. The altitude of a triangle exceeds the base by 4 inches. If the area of the triangle is 30 square inches, the base and altitude of the triangle are _____ and _____ inches, respectively. 6._____
   A. 6; 10 B. 5; 12 C. 2; 6 D. 2; 30

7. The value of $\dfrac{7!}{4!}$ is 7._____
   A. 30 B. 175 C. 210 D. 220

8. If $2x = 3y$ and $4x - 5y = 2$, then x equals 8._____
   A. 6 B. 5 C. 4 D. 3

45

9. Given the points A(-5,-1) and B(3,5), the length of line segment AB is

   A. 6   B. 10   C. 12   D. 25

10. The sum of the interior angles of a polygon with eight sides is

    A. 1260°   B. 1080°   C. 800°   D. 720°

11. Assume that a stairway has 18 risers. Each riser is 7 1/2" high.
    If the floor elevation at the lower level is 102.00 feet, then the floor elevation at the upper level is MOST NEARLY _____ feet.

    A. 109.72   B. 112.10   C. 113.25   D. 114.05

12. The top course of a wall, designed to shed water and to give a finished appearance, is the

    A. jamb   B. saddle
    C. water table   D. coping

13. A map is drawn to a scale of 1" = 30'.
    The type of scale that would indicate distances on this map without further conversion is a(n)

    A. engineers scale   B. architects scale
    C. surveyor's tape   D. yard stick

14. If an isometric drawing has one axis vertical, then the other two axes make an angle with the horizontal equal to

    A. 30°   B. 45°   C. 60°   D. 90°

15. The foundations of a building should be carried below the frost line to prevent

    A. pollution   B. corrosion
    C. asphyxiation   D. heaving

16. Creosote is COMMONLY used as a preservative for

    A. vitrified clay sewers   B. brick walls
    C. PVC pipe   D. timber piles

17. Gaseous chlorine is a greenish-yellow poisonous substance used in the disinfection of water.
    When used for disinfection, its PRIMARY purpose is to

    A. kill bacteria   B. prevent corrosion
    C. filter the water   D. color the water green

18. A bolt has a round head and a square nut. The portion of the shank immediately under the head is square and the remainder of the shank is round.
    This type of bolt is called a _____ bolt.

    A. carriage   B. expansion   C. lag   D. toggle

19. The size of a nail is designated as 8d. This designation means

    A. 8 penny   B. 8 times the diameter
    C. 8 inches   D. 8 centimeters

20. Noxious gases and foul odors are prevented from passing from the sewer to the building drainage pipes by a   20._____

    A. cross connection
    B. goose neck
    C. wye fitting
    D. trap with a water seal

21. While trenches are being excavated, for sewer construction, the earth sides are frequently held in place by   21._____

    A. sheeting
    B. a cradle
    C. slope stakes
    D. batter boards

22. After concrete is poured, it is covered with plastic sheets or wet burlap in order to reduce   22._____

    A. evaporation
    B. vibration
    C. settlement
    D. honeycombing

23. A 1:2:4 concrete consists of 1 part cement to 2 parts fine aggregate and 4 parts   23._____

    A. gypsum
    B. lime
    C. water
    D. coarse aggregate

24. A sewer is laid on a slope of 0.25% between two manholes 180 feet apart. The difference in elevation between the upstream and downstream ends of the sewer is MOST NEARLY _____ feet.   24._____

    A. 0.45 B. 0.60 C. 0.90 D. 1.80

25. A map is drawn to a scale of 1" = 2000'. If 1 acre equals 43,560 square feet, then a 10 inch diameter circle on the map represents an area of MOST NEARLY _____ acres.   25._____

    A. 564 B. 3604 C. 4326 D. 7208

KEY (CORRECT ANSWERS)

1. D
2. C
3. D
4. A
5. D

6. A
7. C
8. D
9. B
10. B

11. C
12. D
13. A
14. A
15. D

16. D
17. A
18. A
19. A
20. D

21. A
22. A
23. D
24. A
25. D

TEST 2

DIRECTIONS: Each question or incomplete statement is followed by several suggested answers or completions. Select the one that BEST answers the question or completes the statement. *PRINT THE LETTER OF THE CORRECT ANSWER IN THE SPACE AT THE RIGHT.*

1. A plan is drawn to a scale of 3/8" = 1'0".
   A line 2 1/2" long on the plan represents a distance of MOST NEARLY _____ feet.

   A. 9.21   B. 8.00   C. 7.33   D. 6.67

   1._____

2. Two gears of different diameters are meshed together. If the larger gear rotates at 100 rpm, the SMALLER gear will rotate

   A. faster
   B. slower
   C. at the same speed
   D. first in one direction, then in the other

   2._____

3. A fence is to be constructed along the property lines of a rectangular tract 60' x 100'. One fence post is to be placed at each corner, and the rest of the posts are to be placed around the periphery, at 10' on centers. Neglecting gates, the number of fence posts required is

   A. 38   B. 36   C. 34   D. 32

   3._____

4. A piece of wood 2 feet thick, 1 foot wide, and 10 feet long weighs 800 pounds. The wood is placed in water weighing 62.4 pounds per cubic foot.
   If the 2-foot-by-10-foot side is parallel to the surface of the water, the 1-foot side will be submerged to a depth of MOST NEARLY _____ inches.

   A. 6.24   B. 7.10   C. 7.39   D. 7.69

   4._____

5. Drawings for a building are made on sheets 36" x 48". There are 120 drawings in a set. If prints cost 6 cents per square foot, the cost for three prints of each of the 120 drawings is MOST NEARLY

   A. $259   B. $230   C. $99   D. $52

   5._____

6. Of the following, the one which would NOT be used for sub-surface examination is

   A. auger borings   B. test pits
   C. core borings   D. stadia measurements

   6._____

7. The diary of a construction project is MOST commonly known as a

   A. log   B. organization chart
   C. bar diagram   D. audit

   7._____

8. On a topographic map, a contour line is a line joining points of EQUAL

   A. temperature   B. distance   C. pressure   D. elevation

   8._____

9. If there are 43,560 square feet in an acre and 640 acres in a square mile, then the number of acres in a tract of land 2640 feet by 7920 feet is MOST NEARLY

   A. 640   B. 480   C. 360   D. 10

   9._____

10. Point B is 3 miles north and 4 miles east of Point A. A person traveling in a straight line from A to B and back again to A would travel a distance EQUAL to _____ miles.

   A. 14   B. 12   C. 10   D. 5

11. The flow from a wide open fire hydrant is 300 gallons per minute. When the hydrant is equipped with a spray nozzle, the flow is reduced to 20 gallons per minute.
Over a period of 8 hours, the quantity of water saved by installing a spray nozzle is MOST NEARLY _____ gallons.

   A. 146,200   B. 134,400   C. 56,500   D. 2,400

12. A rectangular building is 100 feet long and 40 feet wide. Waterproofing is to be applied to the exterior of the 10-foot high basement walls at the rate of 2.5 gallons per 100 square feet of wall.
The number of gallons of waterproofing required is MOST NEARLY

   A. 70   B. 60   C. 28   D. 10

13. An angle is measured 4 times, and the total of the four readings is 186 41' 22". The angle is MOST NEARLY

   A. 47 10' 12.0"   B. 46 40' 20.5"
   C. 46 32' 17.6"   D. 45 30' 15.4"

14. A wood beam spans 20 feet. A man weighing 150 pounds stands 4 feet from the left support, and a man weighing 200 pounds stands 10 feet from the left support. Neglecting the weight of the beam, the reaction at the left support is MOST NEARLY _____ pounds.

   A. 350   B. 250   C. 220   D. 200

15. A car starting from rest accelerates at the rate of 10 ft/sec^2.
At the end _____ of 6 seconds, the distance the car will have traveled is MOST NEARLY _____ feet.

   A. 322   B. 180   C. 155   D. 60

16. The bearing of line EF is S30°W, and the bearing of line EG is N80°W.
The angle CEF is MOST NEARLY

   A. 120°   B. 80°   C. 70°   D. 60°

17. A machine lifts a steel beam weighing 5000 pounds to the top of a building 44 feet high in 40 seconds.
If 55 ft. lbs/sec is equal to one horsepower, the horsepower developed in lifting the beam is MOST NEARLY

   A. 35   B. 24   C. 18   D. 10

18. The distance on a survey line between station 107 + 21.2 and 3 + 72.8 is MOST NEARLY _____ feet.

   A. 7093.4   B. 10347.4   C. 10348.4   D. 10783.9

19. A stone weighs 160 pounds in air and 100 pounds when submerged in water which weighs 62.4 pounds per cubic foot.
    The volume of the stone is MOST NEARLY _____ cubic feet.

    A. 0.44   B. 0.82   C. 0.86   D. 0.96

20. A square tract of land contains 57,600 square feet. The length of a fence needed to enclose the entire property is MOST NEARLY _____ feet.

    A. 960   B. 752   C. 480   D. 300

21. The number of board feet in a piece of wood 1" x 12" x 10' is MOST NEARLY

    A. 0.83   B. 10   C. 12   D. 120

22.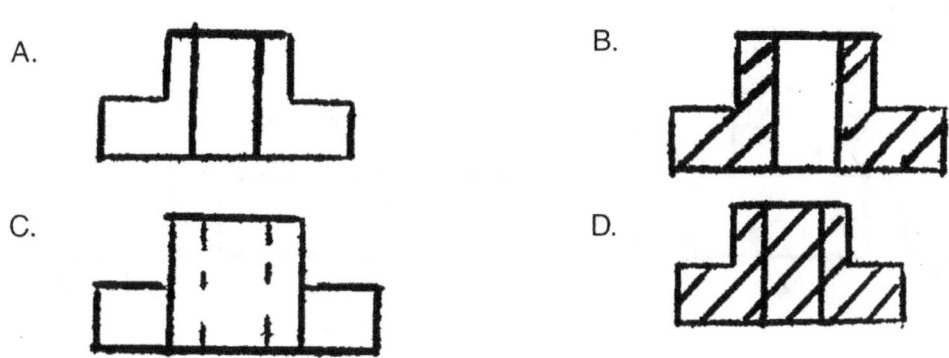

The plan of an object is shown above. Section X - X should be shown as

A.

B.

C.

D.

Questions 23-25.

DIRECTIONS: Questions 23 through 25 are to be answered on the basis of the top view and front elevation of an object as shown at the left. At the right are four drawings, one of which represents the end elevation of the object as seen from the right. Select the drawing which represents the correct end elevation and put the correct letter in the space at the right.

The first group is shown as an example only. The correct answer is B.

4 (#2)

SAMPLE END ELEVATION

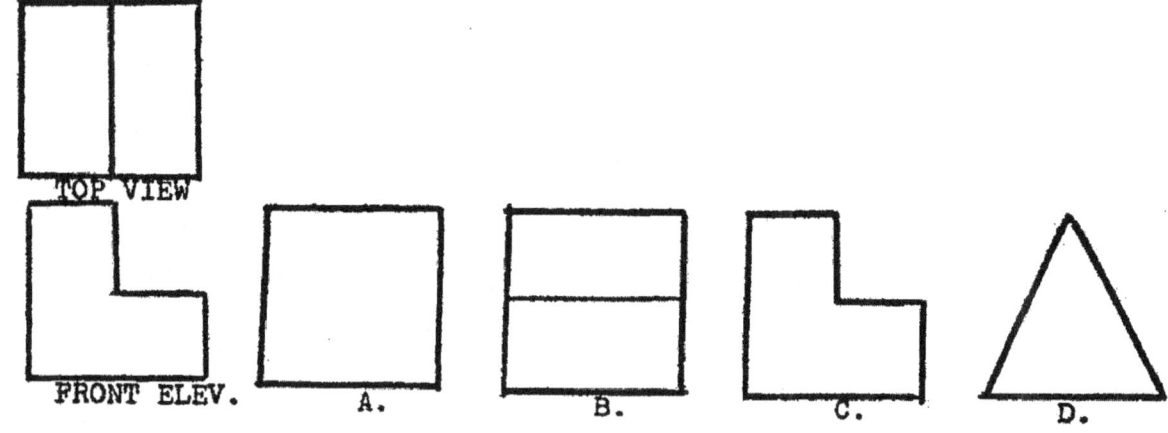

23.

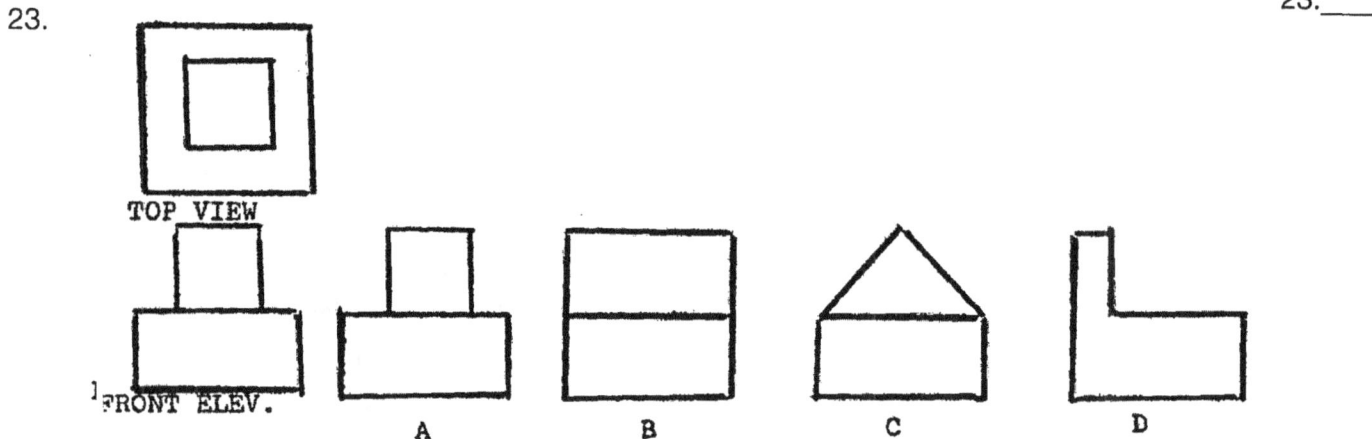

23.____

24.

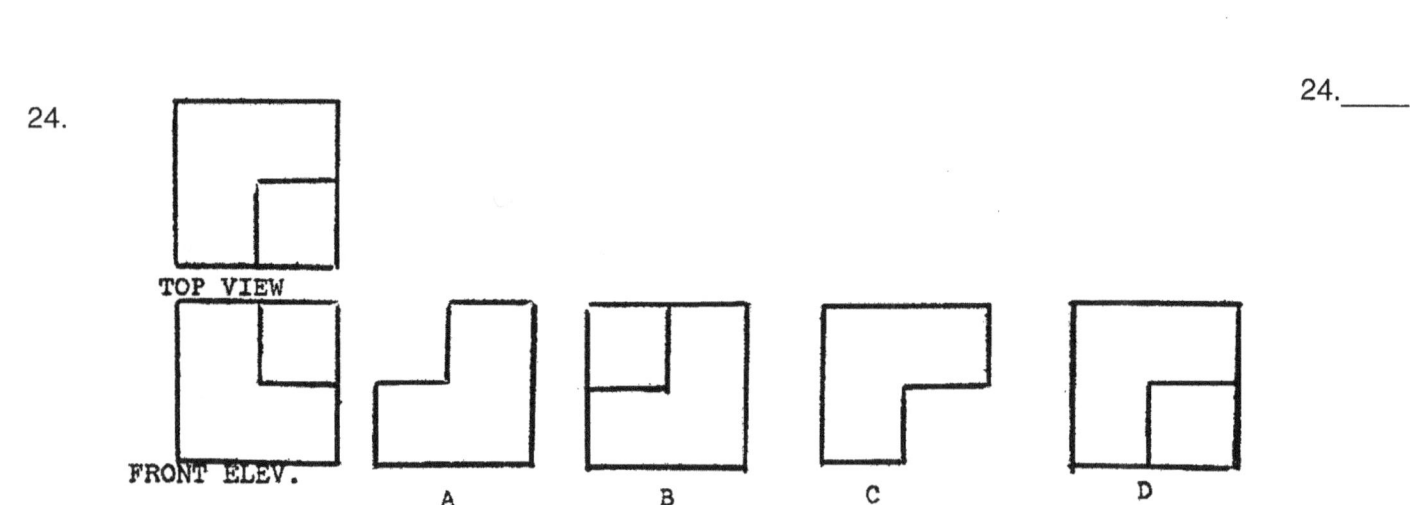

24.____

5 (#2)

25.

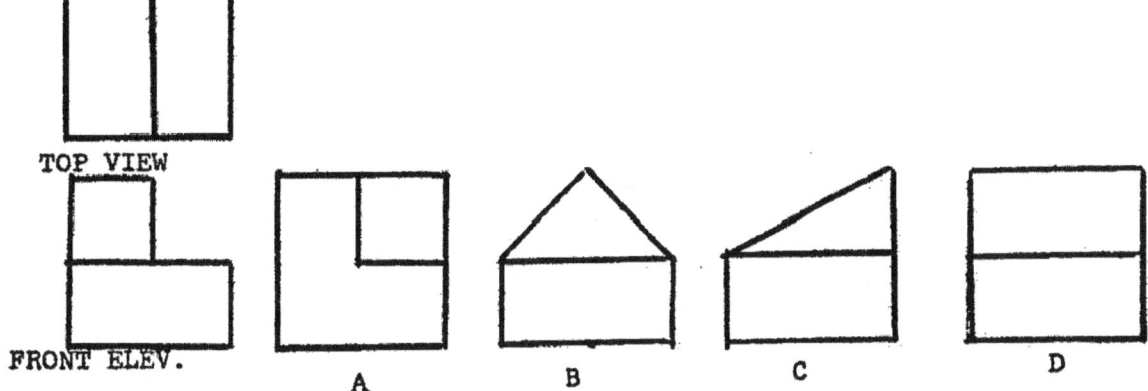

25. ____

KEY (CORRECT ANSWERS)

1. D
2. A
3. D
4. D
5. A

6. D
7. A
8. D
9. B
10. C

11. B
12. A
13. B
14. C
15. B

16. C
17. D
18. C
19. D
20. A

21. B
22. B
23. A
24. B
25. C

EXAMINATION SECTION
TEST 1

DIRECTIONS: Each question or incomplete statement is followed by several suggested answers or completions. Select the one that BEST answers the question or completes the statement. *PRINT THE LETTER OF THE CORRECT ANSWER IN THE SPACE AT THE RIGHT.*

1. Spontaneous combustion is started by the accumulation of heat from slow 1.____

   A. resonance
   B. electrolysis
   C. cooling
   D. oxidation

2. Power may be defined as 2.____

   A. force times distance
   B. mass times acceleration
   C. mass times velocity
   D. the rate of doing work

3. The British thermal unit (BTU) is the amount of heat needed to 3.____

   A. warm one pound of water one Fahrenheit degree
   B. maintain a temperature of 68° F in one pound of water
   C. melt one pound of ice
   D. change one pound of water to steam

4. A temperature of 60° C is, in °F, 4.____

   A. 150   B. 140   C. 120   D. 108

5. An inclined plane 6 feet long and 4 inches high has a *theoretical* mechanical advantage of 5.____

   A. 1.5   B. 10   C. 18   D. 24

6. If the velocity of an object is doubled, its kinetic energy is 6.____

   A. doubled
   B. quadrupled
   C. quartered
   D. halved

7. The volume of a given weight of dry gas is inversely proportional to its pressure, *provided* the temperature 7.____

   A. increases
   B. decreases
   C. remains constant
   D. is within the ambient range

8. Water, at a pressure of one atmosphere (760 mm of mercury), boils at a temperature of 8.____

   A. 460°R   B. 21°F   C. 100°C   D. 4°C

9. The angle of declination is the number of degrees that a compass needle varies from 9.____

   A. the equator
   B. mean sea level
   C. true south
   D. true north

10. If the pressure of a gas is kept constant, the volume will vary _____ the absolute temperature

    A. *inversely* as
    B. *directly* as
    C. *inversely* as the square of
    D. *directly* as the square of

11. A hygrometer is an instrument used to determine

    A. absolute pressure
    B. specific gravity
    C. relative humidity
    D. time

12. The separation of white light into its component colors by means of a triangular glass prism is known as

    A. dispersion
    B. reflection
    C. diffraction
    D. magnification

13. A hydraulic press has a small piston 3/8" in diameter and a large piston 1 1/2" in diameter. If a force of 50 pounds is applied to the small piston, the force on the large piston would be _____ pounds.

    A. 1600   B. 800   C. 200   D. 25

14. Brass is an alloy which consists PRIMARILY of

    A. zinc and copper
    B. beryllium and asbestos
    C. bromine and iron
    D. copper and steel

15. The gases produced by the electrolysis of sodium chloride in water solution are

    A. sulfur dioxide and oxygen
    B. carbon monoxide and helium
    C. hydrogen and chlorine
    D. bromine and methane

16. The chemical symbol for potassium is

    A. K   B. P   C. PO   D. Na

17. Carbon tetrachloride has a specific gravity of 1.6. Water weighs 62.4 pounds per cubic foot.
    The pressure intensity, in pounds per square inch gage, at the bottom of a tank 10 feet deep full of carbon tetrachloride is MOST NEARLY

    A. 6.93   B. 16.0   C. 624.0   D. 997.9

18. The resultant of two 80-l forces acting at right angles to each other is MOST NEARLY _____ pounds.

    A. 0   B. 57   C. 113   D. 160

19. If it requires a force of 40 pounds to drag a 240-pound block of concrete across the floor, then the coefficient of friction is MOST NEARLY

    A. 0.17   B. 0.25   C. 6.0   D. 200

20. If electricity costs 8 cents per kilowatt hour, then the cost of burning twelve 75-watt and five 60-watt bulbs for 10 hours is _____ cents.

    A. 62   B. 88   C. 96   D. 124

21. A steel rail is 60 feet long at 10° C.
    If the coefficient of linear expansion is 0.000013/C°, then the length of the rail, at 50° C, is MOST NEARLY _____ feet.

    A. 59.969   B. 60.003   C. 60.031   D. 62.328

22. A square tank 12 feet high having a perimeter of 40 feet is filled with water weighing 62.4 pounds per cubic foot. The total horizontal force on one side of the tank due to the water pressure is MOST NEARLY _____ pounds.

    A. 58,000   B. 45,000   C. 36,000   D. 13,000

23. A barge 30 feet long and 20 feet wide floats in sea water weighing 64 pounds per cubic foot. The barge sinks 6 inches when a truck is driven aboar
    The weight of the truck is MOST NEARLY _____ pounds.

    A. 21,800   B. 19,200   C. 7,900   D. 6,300

24. Assume that a mercury barometer indicates an atmospheric pressure of 29 inches and that mercury weighs 848 pounds per cubic foot.
    The atmospheric pressure, in pounds per square inch, under these conditions is MOST NEARLY

    A. 15.0   B. 14.7   C. 14.2   D. 13.2

25. An electric iron draws 12 amperes on a 110-volt circuit. If electricity costs 5 cents per kilowatt-hour, the cost to operate the iron for 6 hours is _____ cents.

    A. 40   B. 56   C. 22   D. 110

KEY (CORRECT ANSWERS)

1. D
2. D
3. A
4. B
5. C

6. B
7. C
8. C
9. D
10. B

11. C
12. A
13. B
14. A
15. C

16. A
17. A
18. C
19. A
20. C

21. C
22. B
23. B
24. C
25. A

TEST 2

DIRECTIONS: Each question or incomplete statement is followed by several suggested answers or completions. Select the one that BEST answers the question or completes the statement. *PRINT THE LETTER OF THE CORRECT ANSWER IN THE SPACE AT THE RIGHT.*

1. Ohm's Law states that the intensity of an electric current varies *directly* as the electromotive force and *inversely* as the

    A. potential   B. resistance
    C. voltage   D. energy

    1.____

2. A step-up transformer has a turn ratio of 1 to 20.
   If 110 volts A.C. is applied to the primary, then the voltage on the secondary is _____ volts.

    A. 4400   B. 2200   C. 220   D. 55

    2.____

3. Wire A has a resistance of 30 ohms. Wire B, made of the same material, is the same length as A and has a diameter twice as large as
   The resistance of wire B is _____ ohms.

    A. 60   B. 30   C. 15   D. 7.5

    3.____

4. If an observer sees the flash of a cannon 2 seconds before he hears the sound, the *approximate* distance between the observer and the cannon is _____ feet.

    A. 186,000   B. 10,720   C. 2,180   D. 600

    4.____

5. The pH of vinegar is MOST NEARLY

    A. 212   B. 10^2 C. 12   D. 2.8

    5.____

6. The value of 9 3/4 inches, expressed in feet, is MOST NEARLY

    A. 0.67   B. 0.75   C. 0.813   D. 1.15

    6.____

7. When $\frac{x}{3} - 2$ is subtracted from $\frac{x+6}{3}$, the answer is

    A. 0   B. 2   C. -2   D. 4

    7.____

8. The length of a rectangle is 4 times the width.
   If the area of the rectangle is 324 square feet, the dimensions of the rectangle, in feet, are

    A. 4 x 81   B. 8 x 41   C. 9 x 36   D. 12 x 27

    8.____

9. The reciprocal of $\frac{25x^2}{y}$ is

    A. $-\frac{y}{25x^2}$ B. $-\frac{25x^2}{y}$ C. $\frac{y}{25x^2}$ D. $\frac{25y}{x^2}$

    9.____

10. If $\frac{3a-1}{4} = 2$, then a equals

   A. 2	B. 3	C. 4	D. 9

11. An angle E is 60 degrees larger than its supplement. The number of degrees in angle E is

   A. 270	B. 120	C. 60	D. 30

12. The three angles of a triangle are in the ratio of 2:3:4. If one of the angles is 60°, the other two angles are

   A. 30° and 90°	B. 20° and 100°
   C. 40° and 80°	D. 50° and 70°

13. y varies inversely with x^2. If y = 12 when x = 2, then when x = 4, y is equal to

   A. 2	B. 3	C. 4	D. 6

14. If the base angle of an isosceles triangle is four times the vertex angle, the number of degrees in the vertex angle is

   A. 13	B. 20	C. 27.5	D. 30

15. The angle of a sector of a circle is 160 degrees and the radius of the circle is 12 inches. The area of the sector, in square inches, is

   A. 144π	B. 64π	C. 32π	D. 24π

16. The number 8^6 is the same as the number

   A. 2^{48}	B. 2^{15}	C. 2^{18}	D. 4^{16}

17. Assume that a circle has a radius of 70 feet. The perimeter of this circle is MOST NEARLY _____ feet.

   A. 219.8	B. 439.6	C. 690	D. 15,306

18. The numerical value of $9^{3/2}$ is

   A. 18	B. 27	C. 36	D. 81

19. The numerical value of $\sqrt{640}$ is MOST NEARLY

   A. 80	B. 25.3	C. 24.3	D. 20

20. The number of radians in the arc of a circle whose central angle is 120° is

   A. $2/3\,\pi$	B. π	C. $3/2\,\pi$	D. 4

21. The value of $5\sqrt{12} - 2\sqrt{27}$ is equal to

   A. $4\sqrt{3}$ B. $3\sqrt{5}$ C. $5\sqrt{2}$ D. $3\sqrt{15}$

22. The area of an equilateral triangle whose side is 8 is

   A. 32   B. $16\sqrt{3}$ C. 24   D. $8\sqrt{3}$

23. The logarithm to the base 10 of 1000 is

   A. 100   B. 1.6   C. 2.718   D. 3

24. The cosine of 15° is

   A. $\dfrac{2}{\sqrt{3}}$ B. $\dfrac{\sqrt{3}}{2}$ C. $-\dfrac{1}{2}$ D. $-\dfrac{1}{\sqrt{2}}$

25. The interior angle between two adjacent sides of a regular hexagon is

   A. 180°   B. 120°   C. 90°   D. 60°

KEY (CORRECT ANSWERS)

1. B		11. B	
2. B		12. C	
3. D		13. B	
4. C		14. B	
5. D		15. B	
6. C		16. C	
7. D		17. B	
8. C		18. B	
9. C		19. B	
10. B		20. A	

21. A
22. B
23. D
24. B
25. B

EXAMINATION SECTION
TEST 1

DIRECTIONS: Each question or incomplete statement is followed by several suggested answers or completions. Select the one that BEST answers the question or completes the statement. *PRINT THE LETTER OF THE CORRECT ANSWER IN THE SPACE AT THE RIGHT.*

1. $\sqrt{465}$ is MOST NEARLY

   A. 20.56   B. 21.13   C. 21.34   D. 21.56

2. 90° is MOST NEARLY equal to _____ radians.

   A. 0.5   B. 1.5   C. 2.5   D. 3.5

3. When .68 feet is converted to inches, the result is MOST NEARLY

   A. 7 7/8"   B. 8"   C. 8 1/8"   D. 8 1/4"

4. A 100' guy wire, stretched tight from the top of a vertical pole, makes a 60° angle with the level ground.
   The height of this pole, in feet, is MOST NEARLY (sin 60° = .867, cos 60° = .500)

   A. 50   B. 87   C. 100   D. 200

5. The area of a 120° sector of a circle whose radius is 3" is MOST NEARLY _____ square inches.

   A. 7.9   B. 9.42   C. 11.3   D. 12.5

6. The product $\dfrac{6xy}{x^2 - 4} \cdot \dfrac{5x - 10}{3xy}$ is equal to

   A. $\dfrac{2xy}{x^2 - 40}$ B. $\dfrac{30x^2}{x^2 y}$ C. $\dfrac{10}{x + 2}$ D. $\dfrac{18x^3 y}{x + 10}$

7. The $\sin^2 x$ is equal to

   A. $1 - 2\cos^2 x$
   B. $1 + 2\cos^2 x$
   C. $1 + \cos^2 x$
   D. $1 - \cos^2 x$

8. The volume of a cylinder with a radius of r and height h is

   A. $\pi r^2 h$ B. $2\pi r h$ C. $2\pi r^2 h$ D. $4\pi r^2 h$

9. The expression $\sqrt{28} - \sqrt{7}$ reduces to

   A. $\sqrt{7}$ B. $3\sqrt{7}$ C. $\sqrt{21}$ D. $-\sqrt{35}$

10. If sin 2x = 1, then x is

    A. 30° B. 45° C. 60° D. 75°

11. The expression $\dfrac{x^{-2}y^2}{y} - \dfrac{x^2}{x^4} + y^0$ reduces to

    A. $\dfrac{xy}{x^4}$ B. $\dfrac{y^2}{y-x^4}$ C. $\dfrac{y-1}{x^2+1}$ D. $\dfrac{y-1}{x^2+y}$

12. If the coordinates of E and F in the X-Y plane are (1,-1) and (4,3), respectively, then the length of line E-F is

    A. 4 B. 5 C. 6 D. 7

13. The sum of the interior angles of a regular octagon is

    A. 360° B. 540° C. 1080° D. 1800°

14. The number of cubic yards of concrete required to fill eighteen 24" diameter steel pipe piles 150 feet long is MOST NEARLY

    A. 80 B. 155 C. 315 D. 630

15. A flow of 100 gallons per second for a day is, in millions of gallons per day, MOST NEARLY equal to

    A. 7.93 B. 8.05 C. 8.64 D. 9.20

16. It takes 4 hours for a certain pump to drain an excavation by itself. It takes a second pump 6 hours to drain that same excavation working by itself.
    If both pumps are used together, the length of time it will take to drain the excavation is MOST NEARLY _____ minutes.

    A. 120 B. 144 C. 300 D. 600

17. The area, in square yards, of a trapezoid which has an altitude of 81 feet perpendicular to two parallel sides which are 125 feet and 275 feet long, respectively, is MOST NEARLY

    A. 600 B. 1,800 C. 5,400 D. 10,400

18. The expression $\dfrac{7!}{180}$ reduces to

    A. 28 B. 56 C. 112 D. 224

19. If Log 2 = .3010 and Log 3 = .4771, then Log 324 is MOST NEARLY

    A. 1.9898 B. 2.2094 C. 2.5104 D. 2.6387

20. An isosceles right triangle has a(n) _____ angle. 20.____

    A. obtuse   B. 45°   C. 60°   D. 30°

21. The number of cubic yards of topsoil required to cover a rectangular tract of land 108 feet long by 96 feet wide to a depth of 6 inches is MOST NEARLY 21.____

    A. 192   B. 198   C. 215   D. 230

22. If the payment for steel is 25 cents per pound and a 1-inch-square bar 1 foot long weighs 3.4#, then the payment for a steel bar 2" x 4" in cross section 8' long is 22.____

    A. $8.10   B. $32.80   C. $16.40   D. $54.40

23. Expressed in degrees, 57° - 35' - 20" is MOST NEARLY 23.____

    A. 57.585   B. 57.587   C. 57.589   D. 57.591

24. 24.____

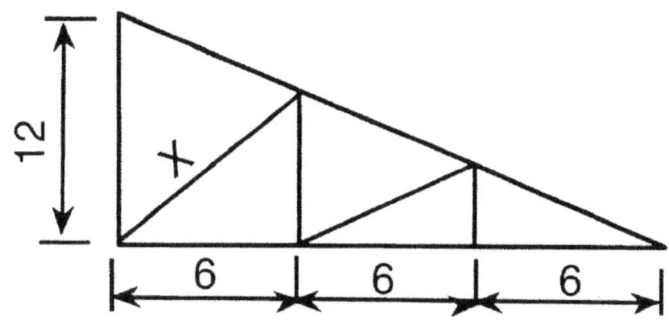

    In the sketch shown above, the length of x is

    A. 8.0   B. 9.0   C. 9.5   D. 10.0

25. In Circle "O," inscribed angle ABC and central angle AOC have the same intercepted arc AC in common. Of the following relationships between angle AOC and angle ABC, the one which is TRUE is that 25.____

    A. angle ABC equals angle AOC
    B. angle AOC equals one-half angle ABC
    C. angle ABC equals one-half angle AOC
    D. nothing can be said about their relative sizes solely on the basis of the information given

KEY (CORRECT ANSWERS)

1.	D	11.	C
2.	B	12.	B
3.	C	13.	C
4.	B	14.	C
5.	B	15.	C
6.	C	16.	B
7.	D	17.	B
8.	A	18.	A
9.	A	19.	C
10.	B	20.	B

21. A
22. D
23. C
24. D
25. C

TEST 2

DIRECTIONS: Each question or incomplete statement is followed by several suggested answers or completions. Select the one that BEST answers the question or completes the statement. *PRINT THE LETTER OF THE CORRECT ANSWER IN THE SPACE AT THE RIGHT.*

1. In pounds per square inch above absolute 0, atmospheric pressure at sea level is MOST NEARLY

    A. 4.7 B. 14.7 C. 19.92 D. 29.92

    1.____

2. Of the following, the one that is a unit in which kinetic energy is expressed is

    A. feet
    B. foot pounds
    C. foot pounds/second
    D. foot pounds per second squared

    2.____

3. The formula for methane gas is

    A. CH_2 B. CH_4 C. C_2H_2 D. C_2H_4

    3.____

4. The substance represented by the formula PbS is known as

    A. galena
    C. zinc blende
    B. caustic soda
    D. litharge

    4.____

5. Of the following statements about water, the one which is TRUE is that

    A. it is practically incompressible
    B. it is most dense at 32° F
    C. a unit volume of water weighs less than the same volume of alcohol
    D. it has no surface tension

    5.____

6. A 50-ohm resistor and a 100-ohm resistor are connected in series to a 120-volt source. Heat will be developed

    A. in the 50-ohm resistor at a greater rate
    B. in the 100-ohm resistor at a greater rate
    C. in both resistors at the same rate
    D. at a greater rate in whichever resistor is connected to the positive side of the voltage source

    6.____

7. An object falling freely from rest for one-half second will drop a distance of MOST NEARLY _____ feet.

    A. 4 B. 8 C. 16 D. 32

    7.____

8. The horsepower required to lift a 2,200-pound weight a vertical distance of 3 feet in one-half second is MOST NEARLY (HP = $\frac{wh}{550}$)

    A. 3 B. 12 C. 24 D. 30

    8.____

65

9. When 2 amps flow through a 20-ohm resistor, the power dissipated by this resistor is MOST NEARLY _____ watts.

   A. 10 B. 20 C. 40 D. 80

10. When the velocity of an object following a circular path is doubled, the centripetal force necessary to keep it in its circular path is

    A. halved
    B. unchanged
    C. doubled
    D. quadrupled

11. The potential difference across a 3-ohm resistor is 12 volts. The current flowing through this resistor is MOST NEARLY _____ amps.

    A. 2 B. 4 C. 6 D. 27

12. The equivalent on the Fahrenheit scale of 100 degrees Centigrade is

    A. $100°$ B. $132°$ C. $180°$ D. $212°$

13. Of the following, the chemical that is an organic compound is

    A. C_6H_6 B. HNO_3 C. H_2SO_3 D. SiO_2

14. A substance which changes the speed of a chemical reaction without itself being permanently changed is known as

    A. amorphous
    B. an amphoteric compound
    C. a catalyst
    D. a salt

15. A chemical reaction accompanied by the evolution of heat is known as

    A. an endothermic reaction
    B. an exothermic reaction
    C. neutralization
    D. nuclear fission

16. The mixing of gases, liquids, and solids by means of molecular motion is called

    A. diffusion
    B. effervescence
    C. decomposition
    D. filtration

17. The ideal mechanical advantage of the pulley system pictured at the right is MOST NEARLY

    A. 2
    B. 3
    C. 4
    D. 5

18. Of the following colors of light, the one with the LONGEST wavelength is

    A. red B. orange C. yellow D. blue

19.

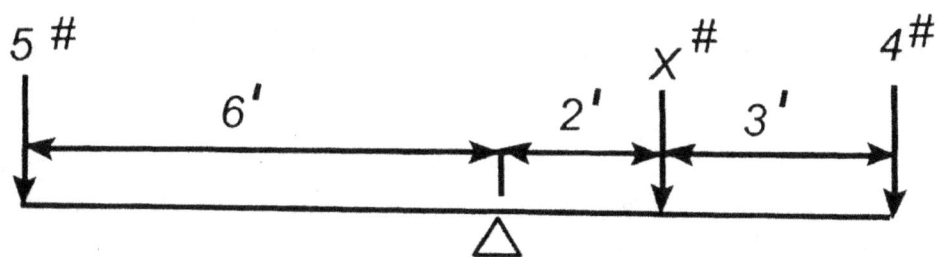

In the lever shown in the sketch above, the magnitude of force X needed to balance the lever is MOST NEARLY _____ lbs.

A. 3.0   B. 4.5   C. 5.0   D. 6.0

20. A 2-candlepower lamp is placed 2 ft. from a photometer screen. Another lamp placed 6 feet from the screen produces equal illumination on the screen.
The illumination of the second lamp is MOST NEARLY _____ cp.

A. 15   B. 18   C. 20   D. 25

21. If, in the diagram shown at the right, the bearing of line OY is S65° E, then the bearing of line OX is

A. S17° E
B. N17° E
C. N17° W
D. S17° W

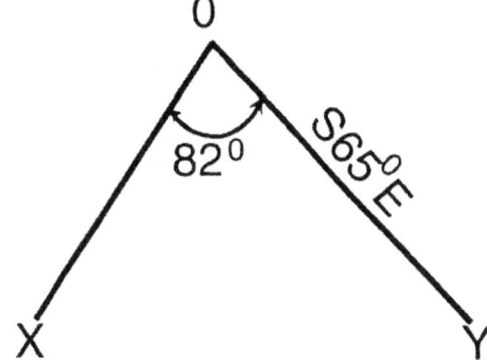

22. If a backsight on a benchmark whose elevation is 116.75' is 8.42' and the foresight on a turning point is 9.35', then the elevation of the turning point is

A. 119.71'   B. 118.53'   C. 117.68'   D. 115.82'

23.

In the closed traverse shown above, the angle X is

A. 33°   B. 40°   C. 47°   D. 55°

24. If a 100-foot-long steel tape contracts 0.00645' upon a temperature drop of 10° F, then the contraction of an 85-foot steel tape for a temperature drop of 65° F is MOST NEARLY

    A. 0.0223'   B. 0.0268'   C. 0.0301'   D. 0.0355'

25. A map made primarily to show relief in ground in such a manner that elevations may be obtained by inspection is known as a(n) _____ map.

    A. planimetric   B. isogonic
    C. railroad   D. topographic

KEY (CORRECT ANSWERS)

1. B		11. B	
2. B		12. D	
3. B		13. A	
4. A		14. C	
5. A		15. B	
6. B		16. A	
7. A		17. A	
8. C		18. A	
9. D		19. C	
10. D		20. B	

21. D
22. D
23. C
24. D
25. D

EXAMINATION SECTION
TEST 1

DIRECTIONS: Each question or incomplete statement is followed by several suggested answers or completions. Select the one that BEST answers the question or completes the statement. *PRINT THE LETTER OF THE CORRECT ANSWER IN THE SPACE AT THE RIGHT.*

1. An empty tank is 6 feet in diameter and 10 feet long. The tank is placed underground in a horizontal position and to a depth where the ground water level is 4 feet above the top of the tank.
   The buoyant force on the tank due to the ground water is MOST NEARLY _____ lbs.

   A. 15,600 B. 16,600 C. 17,600 D. 18,600

2. A wide flange steel beam has a moment of inertia about axis x-x of 3446.5 in.4 and a depth of 27.0 in.
   The section modulus is MOST NEARLY _____ in.^{3}

   A. 240 B. 255 C. 270 D. 285

3. A pump discharges 2 cfs of water weighing 62.4 pcf at a head of 30 feet.
   The output horsepower of the pump is MOST NEARLY _____ HP.

   A. 5.4 B. 6.0 C. 6.8 D. 7.6

4. Water flows through a 6" diameter orifice in the vertical side of a steel tank.
   If the head causing flow is 16 feet, the rate of flow, neglecting losses, is _____ cu.ft./sec.

   A. 6.30 B. 7,30 C. 8.30 D. 9.30

5. A one-inch diameter steel bar, 5 feet long, is subjected to a tensile force of 10,000 pounds.
   If the modulus of elasticity, E, is 30 x 106 psi, the elongation of the bar is _____ in.

   A. .015 B. .025 C. .035 D. .045

6. The charges for water are as follows:
   First   10,000 cu.ft. $3.00/1,000 cu.ft.
   Next   900,000 cu.ft. $2.00/1,000 cu.ft.
   If a customer receives a bill for $90, the quantity of water used is _____ cu.ft.

   A. 40,000 B. 42,000 C. 44,000 D. 46,000

7. The velocity in a 6-inch diameter water pipe is 10 feet per second.
   The velocity in an 8-inch diameter pipe carrying the same discharge is MOST NEARLY _____ ft./sec.

   A. 7.8 B. 13.3 C. 5.6 D. 4.2

8. *WYE-WYE* and *DELTA-WYE* are two

   A. types of D.C. motor windings
   B. types of electrical splices

C. arrangements of 3-phase transformer connections
D. shapes of electrical fuses

9. A beam supporting the masonry over an opening in a wall is a

   A. lintel   B. soffit   C. parapet   D. jamb

10. Very small quantities of fatty acid materials or Vinsol resin are added during the manufacture of portland cement to produce _____ cement.

    A. high-early strength   B. white portland
    C. air-entraining portland   D. oil well

11. When finely divided sand is subjected to the lifting action of water flowing upward through its mass causing it to behave as a liquid, it is called

    A. loam   B. gumbo   C. peat   D. quicksand

12. Wood piles are impregnated with creosote PRIMARILY to

    A. improve appearance   B. prevent fires
    C. reduce decay   D. increase conductivity

13. A method used for placing concrete under water is the _____ method.

    A. auger   B. wellpoint   C. needle   D. tremie

14. A beam resting on the top chord of a roof truss and supporting the rafters or other roof construction is called a

    A. purlin   B. spandrel
    C. lintel   D. grade beam

15. A type of brick bond in which every sixth course of stretcher bond is made a header course is _____ bond.

    A. English   B. Flemish   C. common   D. cross

16. The side member of a window or door opening is called a

    A. sill   B. saddle   C. head   D. jamb

17. Wood members, 2 in. x 4 in., installed 16 inches on center in a wood-frame dwelling are called

    A. rafters   B. sills   C. joists   D. studs

18. A concrete beam which is placed under initial stress by tensioning the steel wires comprising the reinforcement prior to its receiving any stress due to the dead or live load is called a

    A. eb joist   B. prestressed beam
    C. plate girder   D. laminated beam

19. Vermiculite is a lightweight aggregate which is mixed with gypsum to form a

    A. fire-resistant coating   B. flashing
    C. membrane waterproofing   D. non-expansion joint

20. When stucco is applied in three coats, the coats are usually called the finish coat, the brown coat, and the _____ coat.   20._____

    A. earth   B. sheathing   C. scratch   D. mullion

KEY (CORRECT ANSWERS)

1.	C	11.	D
2.	B	12.	C
3.	C	13.	D
4.	A	14.	A
5.	B	15.	C
6.	A	16.	D
7.	C	17.	D
8.	C	18.	B
9.	A	19.	A
10.	C	20.	C

TEST 2

DIRECTIONS: Each question or incomplete statement is followed by several suggested answers or completions. Select the one that BEST answers the question or completes the statement. *PRINT THE LETTER OF THE CORRECT ANSWER IN THE SPACE AT THE RIGHT.*

1. The angle between the *true* meridian and the *magnetic* meridian is called the   1._____

   A. zimuth
   B. bearing
   C. magnetic declination
   D. longitude

2. A scale of 1/24000 is the same as a scale of   2._____

   A. one-quarter inch equals one foot
   B. 1 inch equals 2000 feet
   C. 1 inch equals 1 mile
   D. 1 foot equals 5000 feet

Questions 3-4.

DIRECTIONS: Questions 3 and 4 refer to the following notes on surveying leveling.

STA.	B.S.	H.I.	F.S.	Elev.
BM1	6.42	124.66		
TE1	5.88		1.63	
BM2			10.20	

3. The elevation of BM1 is MOST NEARLY   3._____

   A. 111.82   B. 118.24   C. 122.46   D. 125.78

4. The elevation of BM2 is MOST NEARLY   4._____

   A. 136.71   B. 124.62   C. 118.71   D. 112.11

5. The bearing of line AE is N24°-30'E, and the bearing of line AG is S12-0'E.   5._____
   The angle EAG is

   A. 36°-30'   B. 53°-30'   C. 78°-00'   D. 143°-30'

6. A horizontal angle is measured four times by repetition using a transit.   6._____
   If the horizontal plate reads 181°29'44", the angle is

   A. 45°22'26"   B. 46°13'27"   C. 54°12'13"   D. 61°18'12"

7. The distance between two points on the ground was found to be 1246.22 feet when measured with a nominal 50 foot steel tape that was actually 49.95 feet long.   7._____
   The ACTUAL distance between the two points is _____ ft.

   A. 1244.67   B. 1245.22   C. 1247.22   D. 1248.14

8. An 8-inch diameter sewer is laid on a slope of 0.42% between two manholes 300 feet apart.
If the invert elevation at the upper end is 126.42 feet, the invert elevation at the lower end is _____ ft.

   A. 126.01   B. 125.94   C. 125.36   D. 125.16

9. A temperature of 100 degrees Fahrenheit is MOST NEARLY equal to _____ degrees C.

   A. 32   B. B,38   C. 112   D. 212

10. A square tank 10 feet wide and 12 feet high is filled with water weighing 62.4 pounds per cubic foot.
The horizontal hydrostatic force on one side of the box is MOST NEARLY _____ lbs.

    A. 40,000   B. 45,000   C. 50,000   D. 55,000

11. Dry ice is made from

    A. hydrogen sulfide   B. carbon dioxide
    C. calcium oxide   D. sodium chloride

12. The chemical symbol for silver is

    A. Ag   B. Au   C. Si   D. Se

13. Natural gas consists of *approximately* 90 percent

    A. chlorine   B. acetylene   C. oxygen   D. methane

14. Of the following, the instrument used to measure the specific gravity of the solution in an automobile battery is a(n)

    A. hygrometer   B. pyrometer
    C. hydrometer   D. radiometer

15. A circuit contains three 10-ohm resistors in series.
The COMBINED equivalent resistance of the three resistors is _____ ohms.

    A. 1/30   B. 1/10   C. 10   D. 30

16. A car starting from rest accelerates at the rate of 8 ft./sec.^{2}
At the end of 6 seconds, the car will have traveled a distance equal to _____ feet.

    A. 144   B. 136   C. 120   D. 94

17. A bag of cement estimated at 0.875 cubic foot of volume contains a net weight of cement equal to _____ lbs.

    A. 56   B. 78   C. 94   D. 112

18. The contractor shall regulate the consistency of the mix to the slump directed by the engineer.
Such a statement is part of a specification for

    A. concrete   B. asphalt
    C. gravel   D. top soil

19. Mortar briquettes composed of one part of Portland cement and three parts of Standard Ottawa sand are USUALLY used for _____ strength tests.   19._____

    A. torsion   B. compression
    C. impact   D. tensile

20. The contractor shall submit to the engineer a CPM Construction Plan. In such a statement, CPM is an abbreviation for   20._____

    A. Control Path Method   B. Critical Path Month
    C. Critical Path Method   D. Control Per Month

KEY (CORRECT ANSWERS)

1.	C	11.	B
2.	B	12.	A
3.	B	13.	D
4.	C	14.	C
5.	D	15.	D
6.	A	16.	A
7.	B	17.	C
8.	D	18.	A
9.	B	19.	D
10.	B	20.	C

EXAMINATION SECTION
TEST 1

DIRECTIONS: Each question or incomplete statement is followed by several suggested answers or completions. Select the one that BEST answers the question or completes the statement. *PRINT THE LETTER OF THE CORRECT ANSWER IN THE SPACE AT THE RIGHT.*

Questions 1-9.

DIRECTIONS: In Questions 1 through 9, inclusive, the front and top view of a solid object is shown. Indicate the correct right side view.

1.

Top View

Front View

(A) (B) (C) (D)

1.____

2.

Top View

Front View

(A) (B) (C) (D)

2.____

75

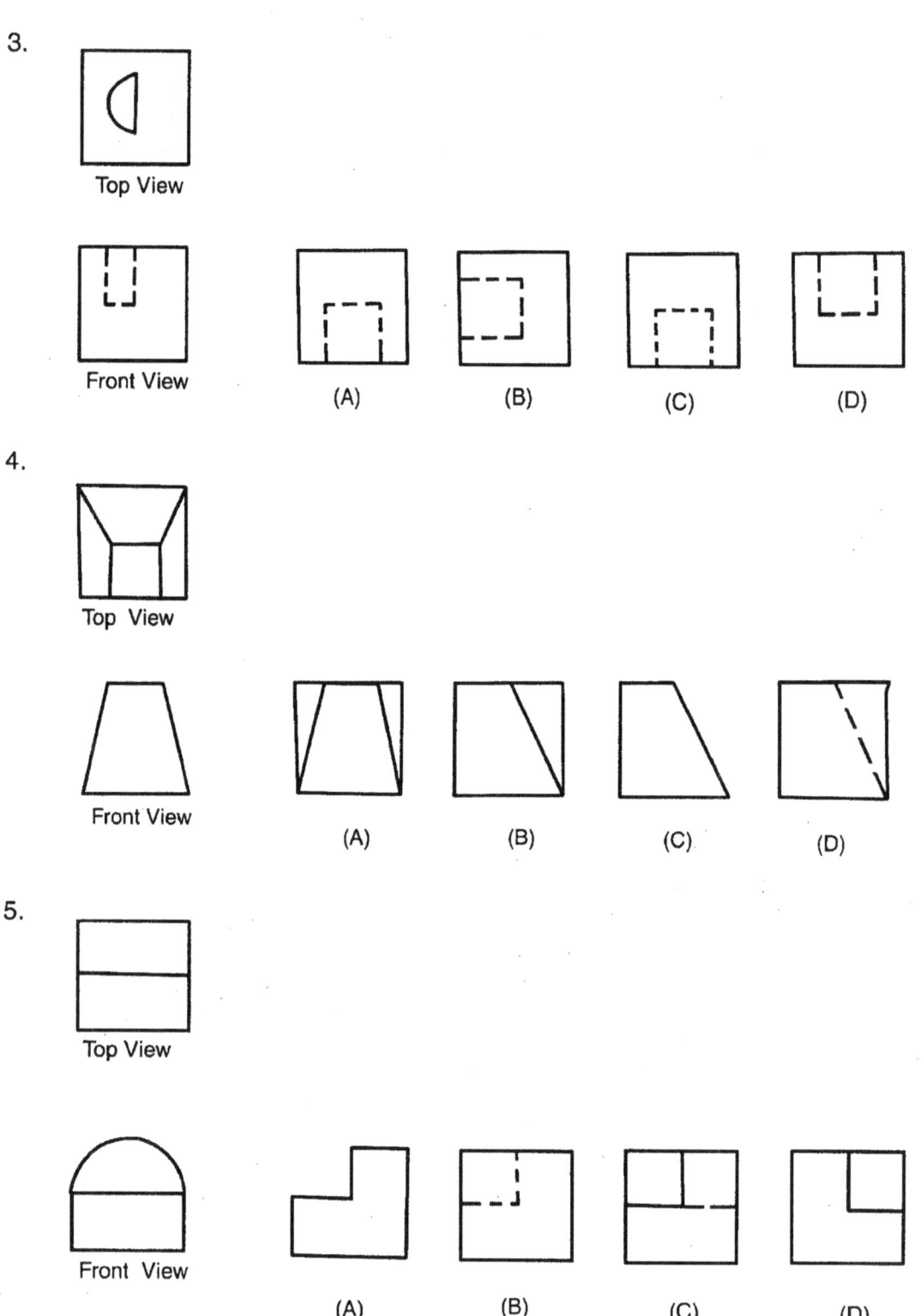

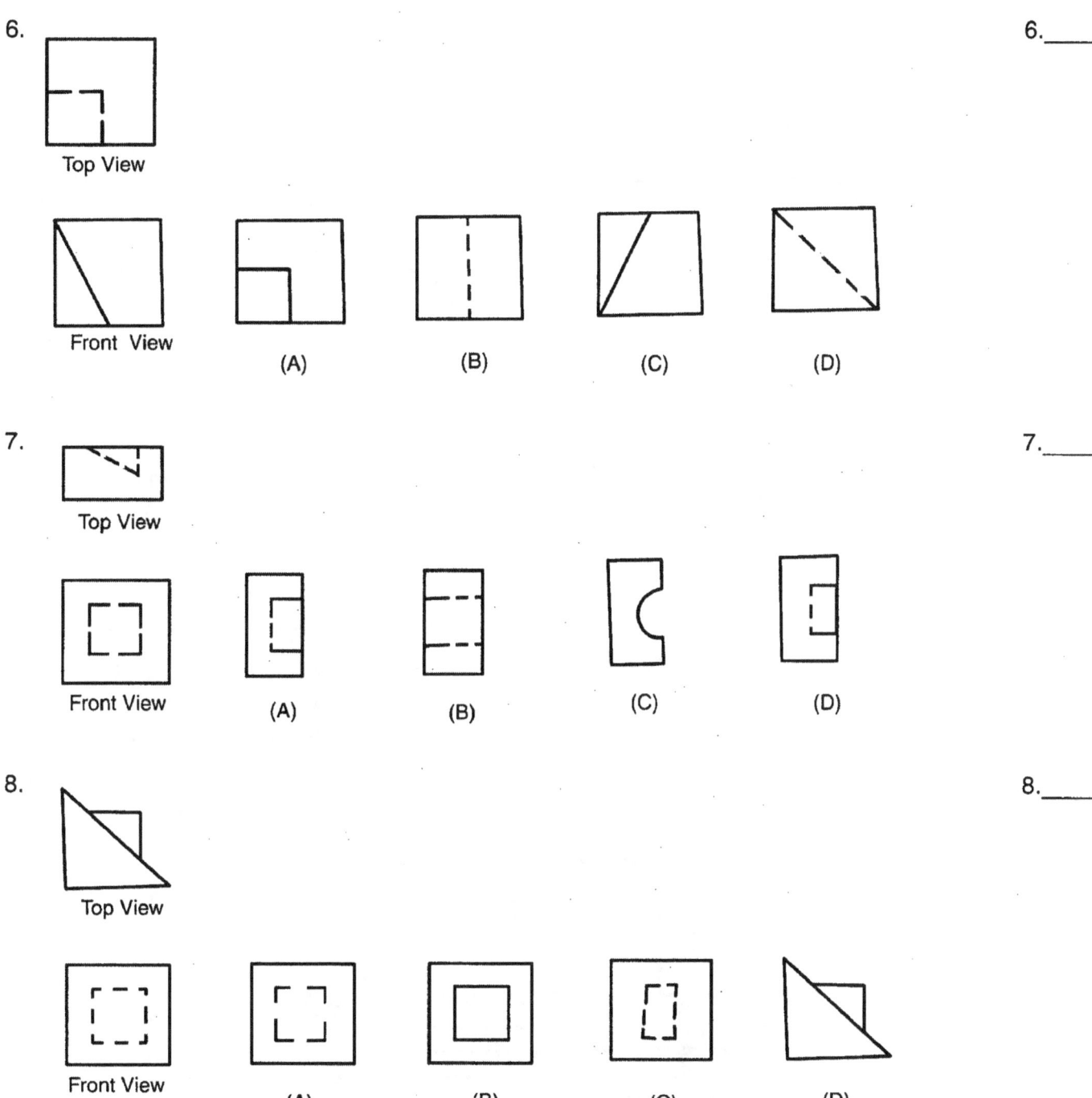

9.

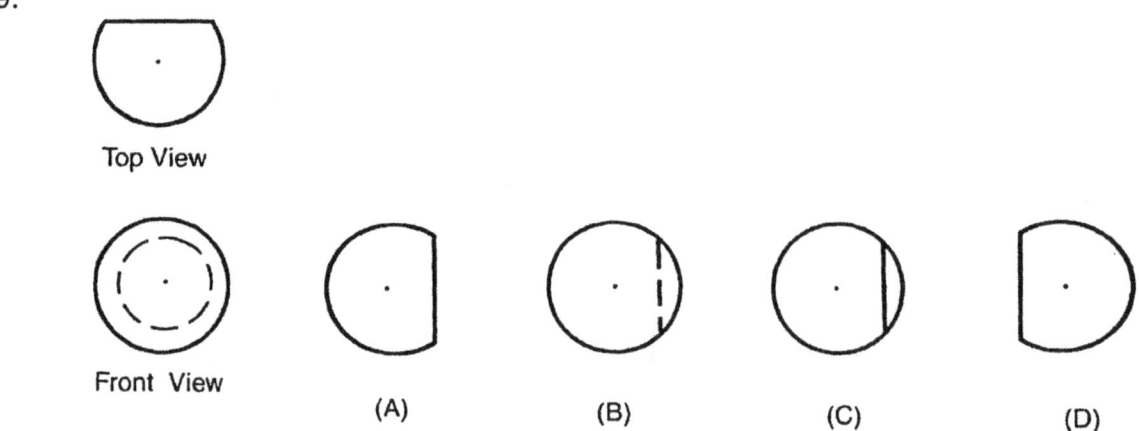

Questions 10-16.

DIRECTIONS: Questions 10 through 16 refer to the partial plan and beam detail shown below.

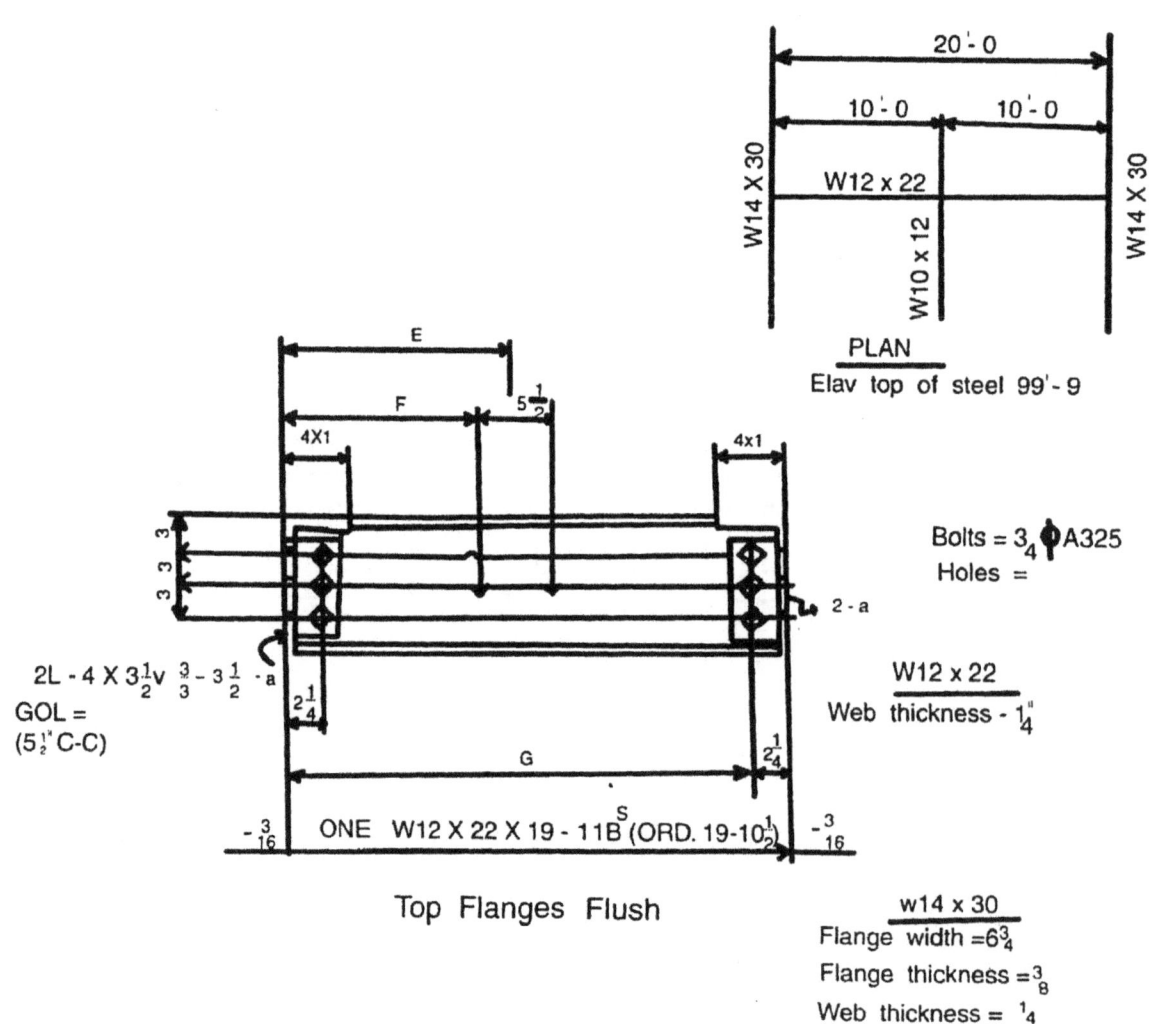

10. Dimension E is

    A. 9'11 11/16" B. 9'11 3/4"
    C. 9'11 13/16" D. 9'11 7/8"

11. Dimension F is

    A. 9'8 15/16" B. 9'9"
    C. 9'9 1/16"   D. 9'9 1/8"

12. Dimension G is

    A. 9'9 3/16" B. 9'9 1/4"
    C. 9'9 5/16" D. 9'9 3/8"

13. The diameter of the holes for the $\frac{3}{4}\phi$ bolts is usually

    A. 25/32"   B. 13/16"   C. 27/32"   D. 7/8"

14. The reason the top of the flange is cut is to

    A. avoid interference with the top flange of the W14x30 beams
    B. avoid interference with the web of the W14x30
    C. facilitate tightening the bolts fastening the angles to the web of the W12x22
    D. facilitate swinging the beam between the two flanges of the W14x30

15. GOL is the abbreviation for gauge on the outstanding leg.
    The GOL for the $L4x3\frac{1}{2}x3/8$ is

    A. 2 7/16"   B. 2 1/2   C. 2 9/16"   D. 2 5/8"

16. The grip of a bolt is the sum of the thicknesses of the material being bolted. The grip for the 3/4-inch bolts shown is

    A. 7/8"   B. 15/16"   C. 1"   D. 1 1/8"

17. Drafting pencils are graded by hardness. Of the following grades of pencils, the one that is the hardest is

    A. H   B. HB   C. F   D. B

18. When lettering with inclined letters, the angle of incline from the horizontal is, in degrees, most nearly

    A. 58   B. 60   C. 67   D. 85

Questions 19-22.

DIRECTIONS: Questions 19 through 22, inclusive, refer to a portion of a map shown below.

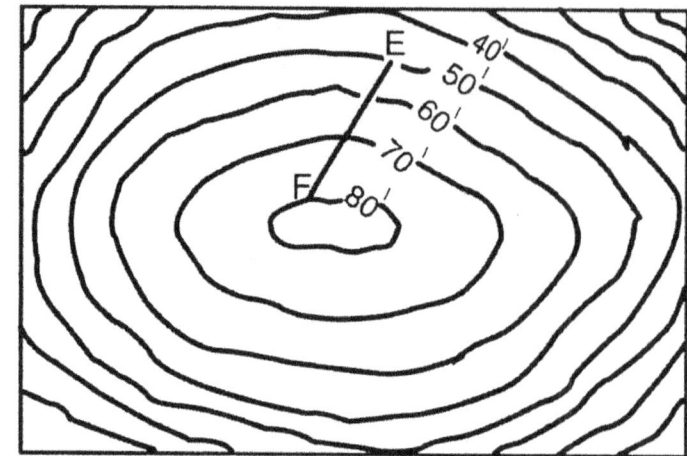

19. This map is called a

    A. detail map
    B. plot plan
    C. topographic map
    D. profile

20. Each closed curve is called a(n)

    A. ellipse
    B. profile
    C. horizontal section
    D. contour

21. This map shows a

    A. defile
    B. uniform grade
    C. valley
    D. hill

22. If the horizontal distance between E and F is 500', the average slope of EF is, in percent, most nearly

    A. 5   B. 6   C. 7   D. 8

23. A 5H lead pencil would most likely be used to draw

    A. invisible lines
    B. the outline of objects
    C. guide lines for lettering
    D. center lines of objects

24. The type of weld shown at the right is a _____ weld.
    A. butt
    B. fillet
    C. field
    D. bevel

25. A drawing has a scale of 3/16" = 1'0". A distance of 50 feet would be _____ in length.

    A. 9 3/8"   B. 9 7/16"   C. 9 1/2"   D. 9 9/16"

KEY (CORRECT ANSWERS)

1. D
2. D
3. D
4. C
5. A

6. B
7. A
8. B
9. A
10. C

11. C
12. D
13. B
14. A
15. D

16. C
17. A
18. C
19. C
20. D

21. D
22. B
23. C
24. B
25. A

TEST 2

DIRECTIONS: Each question or incomplete statement is followed by several suggested answers or completions. Select the one that BEST answers the question or completes the statement. *PRINT THE LETTER OF THE CORRECT ANSWER IN THE SPACE AT THE RIGHT.*

1. A rectangle 16"x35" is drawn on a sheet of paper. Of the following, the best way to insure that the rectangle is truly a rectangle is to 1._____

   A. measure the angles with a protractor to insure they are 90°
   B. check that the opposite sides are equal in length
   C. use a parallel ruler to check that the opposite sides are parallel
   D. check that the diagonals are equal in length

2. Of the following, the one that is an ore used to manufacture steel is 2._____

   A. hematite   B. galena   C. cinnebar   D. bauxite

3. Galvanized steel is steel coated with a layer of 3._____

   A. zinc   B. copper   C. tin   D. lead

4. Of the following types of lumber, the one most commonly used in the frame of a wood-framed house is 4._____

   A. spruce   B. pine   C. oak   D. cedar

5. In making a sidewalk, the procedure that provides a rough even surface that needs further finishing is 5._____

   A. vibrating   B. floating
   C. screeding   D. pointing

6. The ingredients that are used to make Portland cement concrete are usually Portland cement, _____, and water. 6._____

   A. crushed limestone
   B. crushed granite, sand
   C. gravel, trap rock
   D. crushed slag, sand

7. The strength of a concrete mix depends primarily upon the 7._____

   A. ratio of coarse aggregate to fine aggregate
   B. ratio of water to cement
   C. fineness of the sand
   D. maximum size of the coarse aggregate

8. Common brick is usually composed of clay 8._____

   A. only   B. and sand
   C. sand and cement   D. and cement

9. The size of common brick is usually

   A. 2 1/4" x 3 3/4" x 8"
   B. 2 1/2" x 3 3/4" x 7 3/4"
   C. 2 1/4" x 3 1/2" x 8"
   D. 2 1/4" x 3 1/2" x 7 3/4"

10. Mortar for brickwork is usually composed of Portland cement, _____, and water.

    A. sand
    B. sand, lime
    C. lime
    D. slag, lime

11. Some building codes require that for retaining walls and other types of walls, the bottom of the concrete foundations for these walls shall be at least four feet below the ground surface. Of the following, the best reason for this requirement is

    A. the bottom of the footing shall be below the frost line
    B. to minimize settlement
    C. to prevent overturning
    D. to insure that lateral movement of the footing will be minimized

12. The slump test for a concrete mix is to take a sample of the concrete from the mixer, fill a cone with the sample, empty the cone, and measure the slump as shown at the right. The purpose of this test is to determine the _____ of the mix.

    A. economy
    B. porosity
    C. workability
    D. density

13. The minimum thickness of a concrete sidewalk is, in inches, most nearly

    A. 3   B. 4   C. 5   D. 6

14. The bituminous material in an asphalt mix is derived primarily from

    A. natural asphalt deposits
    B. the distillation of crude oil
    C. the distillation of bituminous coal
    D. preparation of coke used in steel manufacture

15. Terrazzo is a material used in

    A. walls
    B. ceilings
    C. floors
    D. the exterior of buildings

16. The Greek symbol for the letter gamma is

    A. α B. β C. γ D. δ

17. One-eighth of an inch as a decimal of a foot is most nearly

    A. .01   B. .02   C. .03   D. .04

18. The cotangent of is
    A. a/c
    B. a/b
    C. b/a
    D. c/a

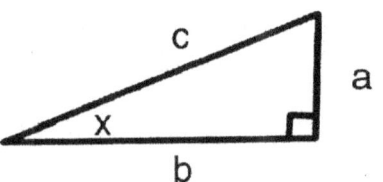

19. The hypotenuse of the right angle triangle shown at the right is
    A. 25
    B. 26
    C. 27
    D. 28

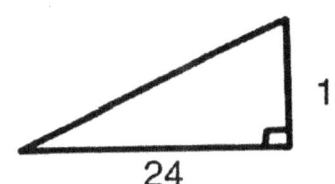

20. The interior angle of a regular hexagon is, in degrees,
    A. 110   B. 120   C. 130   D. 140

21. The area of the rhombus shown at the right is, in square feet, most nearly
    A. 72
    B. 80
    C. 88
    D. 96

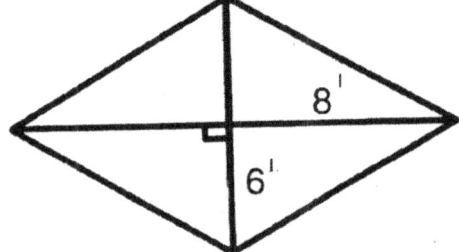

22. The area of the quadrilateral shown at the right is, in square feet, most nearly
    A. 210
    B. 220
    C. 230
    D. 240

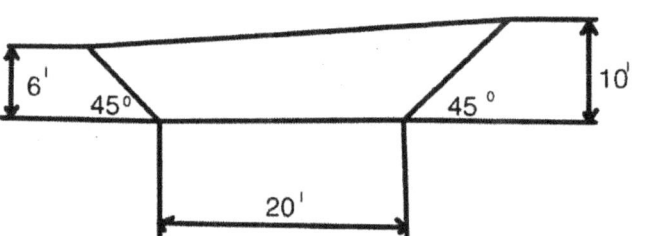

23. The $\text{Log}_{10} 5$ is equal to

    A. $-\text{Log}_{10} 2$ B. 1/5
    C. $1 - \text{Log}_{10} 2$ D. $1 - \text{Log}_{10} 5$

24. Arc sin 1/2 equals

    A. cos 30°   B. cos 60°   C. tan 30°   D. 30°

25. Given the right angled triangle GEH, the magnitude of EF is most nearly

   A. $\dfrac{5\sqrt{3}}{2}$
   B. 5
   C. $5\sqrt{3}$
   D. $\dfrac{5}{\sqrt{3}}$

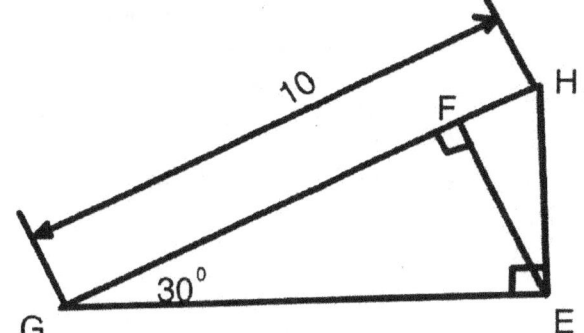

KEY (CORRECT ANSWERS)

1. D
2. A
3. A
4. B
5. C

6. A
7. B
8. A
9. A
10. B

11. A
12. C
13. B
14. B
15. C

16. C
17. A
18. C
19. A
20. B

21. D
22. B
23. C
24. D
25. A

TEST 3

DIRECTIONS: Each question or incomplete statement is followed by several suggested answers or completions. Select the one that BEST answers the question or completes the statement. *PRINT THE LETTER OF THE CORRECT ANSWER IN THE SPACE AT THE RIGHT.*

1. The shaded area shown at the right is

   A. $\dfrac{50}{3}\pi - 50\sqrt{3}$

   B. $\dfrac{25}{3}\pi - 25\sqrt{3}$

   C. $\dfrac{50}{3}\pi - 25\sqrt{3}$

   D. $\dfrac{25}{3}\pi - \dfrac{50\sqrt{3}}{3}$

   1.____

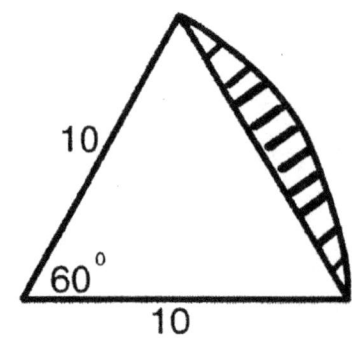

2.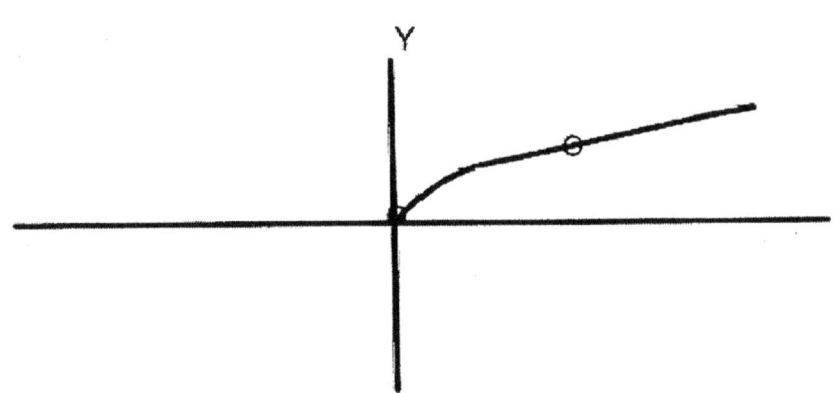

   The above curve is a parabola. Its equation is y =

   A. x^2 B. $-x^2$ C. $-\sqrt{x}$ D. $+\sqrt{x}$

   2.____

3. The shaded area enclosed by the straight line y = 4 - x/2 and the x and y axes is
   A. 10
   B. 12
   C. 14
   D. 16

   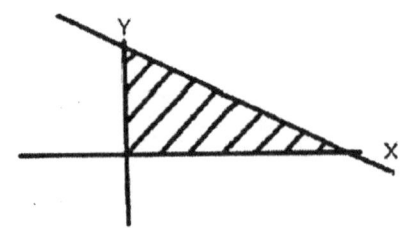

   3.____

4. $(\sqrt{a}+\sqrt{b})^2$ is equal to a + b +

   A. $2\sqrt{ab}$ B. $\sqrt{ab}$ C. 2ab   D. ab

   4.____

5. The angle bisectors of a triangle meet at a point that is

    A. the center of a circle in which the triangle is inscribed
    B. equidistant from the sides of the triangle
    C. the center of gravity of the triangle
    D. equidistant from the vertices of the triangle

6. The area of the trapezoid shown at the right is

    A. $70\sqrt{3}$

    B. $75\sqrt{3}$

    C. $80\sqrt{3}$

    D. $85\sqrt{3}$

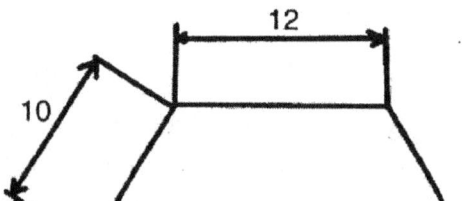

7. The $\tan^2 45° + \sin^2 45°$ is equal to

    A. 3/4   B. 3/2   C. 2   D. 5/2

8. $\cos(90° + x)$ is equal to

    A. $\cos x$ B. $-\cos x$ C. $\sin x$ D. $-\sin x$

9. $\sqrt[3]{1331}$ is equal to

    A. 7   B. 9   C. 11   D. 13

10. 90° in radians is

    A. $\dfrac{\pi}{3}$ B. $\dfrac{\pi}{2}$ C. π D. $\dfrac{3}{2}\pi$

11. $4^4 = 2^x$ x is equals to

    A. 6   B. 8   C. 10   D. 12

12. The slope of the line $\dfrac{x}{3} + \dfrac{y}{4} = 1$ is

    A. 4/3   B. -4/3   C. 3/4   D. -3/4

13. The roots of the equation $x^2 + x - 42 = 0$ are

    A. real and unequal   B. imaginary
    C. irrational   D. real and equal

14. The Toricelli experiment demonstrated that
    A. air has weight
    B. nature abhors a vacuum
    C. the specific gravity of mercury is 13.6
    D. mercury does not adhere to glass

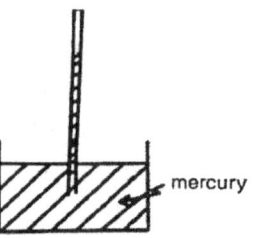

14.____

15. Benjamin Franklin's experiment with a kite during a storm demonstrated that

    A. wire is an electrical conductor
    B. thunder and lightning are related
    C. lightning originates in the clouds
    D. lightning is electrical in nature

15.____

16. Neglecting friction, the force P needed to hold the 240# load in place is, in pounds, most nearly
    A. 60
    B. 80
    C. 100
    D. 120

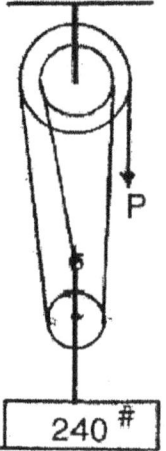

16.____

17. The load P needed to balance the two 20 pound loads is, in pounds, most nearly
    A. 18
    B. 20
    C. 22.5
    D. 25

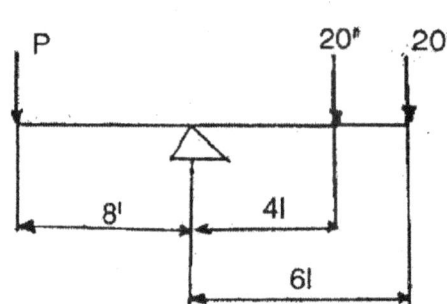

17.____

18. A cube of wood one foot on each side floats in water at a depth of 8 inches. If water weighs 62.4 pounds per cubic foot, the weight of the wood in air is, in pounds, most nearly
    A. 36.8
    B. 38.4
    C. 40
    D. 41.6

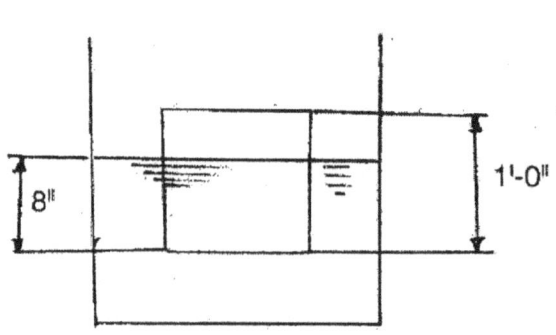

18.____

19. One degree Fahrenheit is equal to _____ degree Centigrade.   19.____
    A. 9/5   B. 5/9   C. 2/3   D. 3/2

20. If water weighs 62.4 pounds per cubic foot, the horizontal force acting on one foot of the dam's length is, in pounds, most nearly   20.____
    A. 500
    B. 530
    C. 560
    D. 600

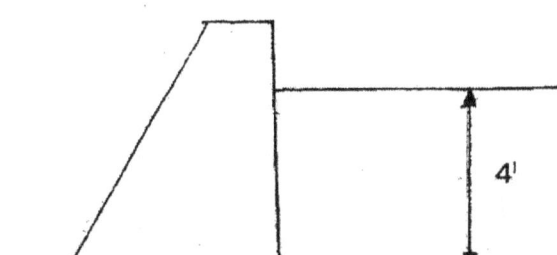

21. An object at rest is dropped from a tall building. Neglecting friction, its downward speed at the end of two seconds would be, most nearly, in feet per second,   21.____
    A. 48   B. 64   C. 80   D. 96

22. The boiling point of water is, in degrees Fahrenheit,   22.____
    A. 100   B. 180   C. 212   D. 252

23. 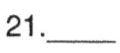 in electronic work, the symbol shown represents   23.____
    A. capacitance   B. inductance
    C. resistance   D. rectifier

24.   24.____

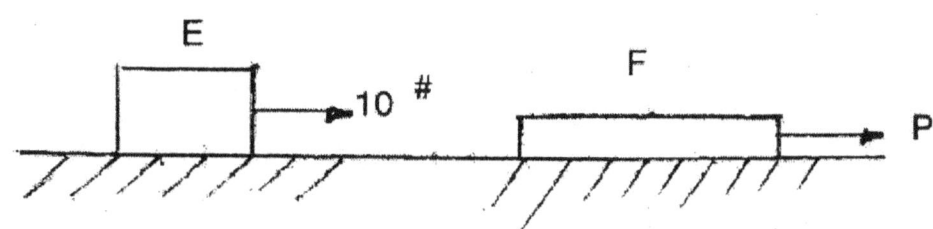

Both objects are of the same material and have the same weight. Object F has 4 times the area of object E in contact with the supporting surface. If object E requires 10 pounds to overcome friction, P is equal to, in pounds,

   A. 2.5   B. 10   C. 15   D. 40

25. An object under the influence of gravity is moving upward with a velocity of 32 feet per second. Neglecting friction, after two seconds, its velocity will be   25.____
    A. 16 feet per second upward
    B. 0
    C. 16 feet per second downward
    D. 32 feet per second downward

KEY (CORRECT ANSWERS)

1. C
2. D
3. D
4. A
5. B

6. D
7. B
8. D
9. C
10. B

11. B
12. B
13. A
14. A
15. D

16. B
17. D
18. D
19. B
20. A

21. B
22. C
23. B
24. B
25. D

TEST 4

DIRECTIONS: Each question or incomplete statement is followed by several suggested answers or completions. Select the one that BEST answers the question or completes the statement. *PRINT THE LETTER OF THE CORRECT ANSWER IN THE SPACE AT THE RIGHT.*

1. Torque may be measured in 1.____
   A. pounds B. kilograms
   C. pound feet D. yards

2. 120 revolutions per minute is, in radians per second, 2.____
   A. π B. 2π C. 4π D. 8π

3. One inch is, in centimeters, 3.____
   A. 2.34 B. 2.44 C. 2.54 D. 2.64

4. One meter is, in inches, most nearly 4.____
   A. 39.37 B. 40.37 C. 41.37 D. 42.37

5. One kilogram is equal to _____ pounds. 5.____
   A. 1.6 B. 1.8 C. 2.0 D. 2.2

6. One kilometer is most nearly equal to _____ miles. 6.____
   A. 0.60 B. 0.65 C. 0.70 D. 0.75

7. A millimeter is equal to _____ meter(s). 7.____
   A. 0.1 B. 0.01 C. 0.001 D. 0.0001

8. A hectare is a measure of 8.____
   A. area B. density C. velocity D. acceleration

9. The number of grams in a pound is most nearly 9.____
   A. 433.6 B. 443.6 C. 453.6 D. 463.6

10. Structural steel is iron with the addition of a small amount of 10.____
    A. tungsten B. carbon C. nickel D. chromium

11. The type of beam shown at the right is called a(n) _____ beam. 11.____
    A. indeterminate
    B. cantilever
    C. fixed end
    D. unstable

12. The reaction at E is, in pounds, most nearly
    A. 25
    B. 30
    C. 40
    D. 50

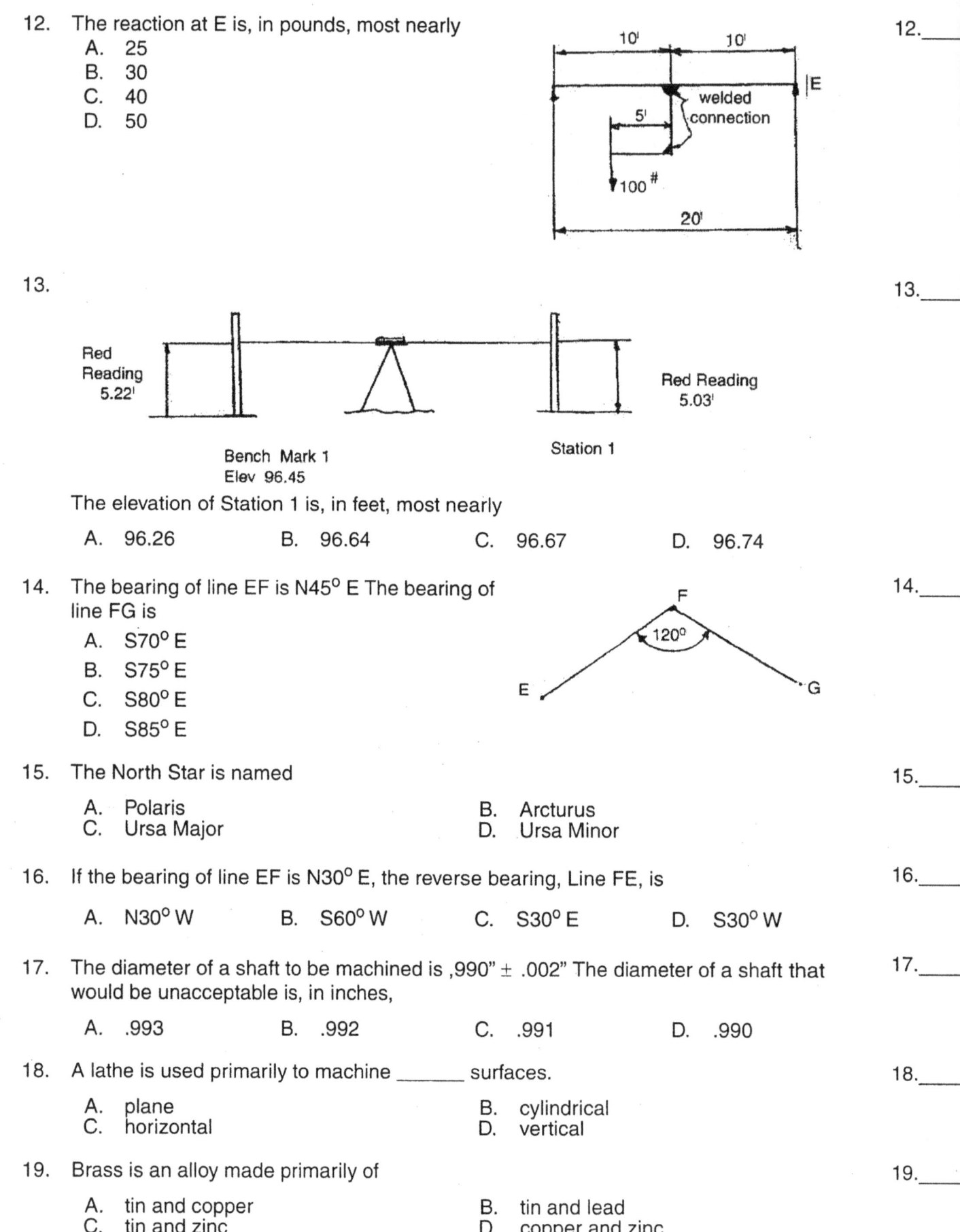

13. The elevation of Station 1 is, in feet, most nearly

    A. 96.26   B. 96.64   C. 96.67   D. 96.74

14. The bearing of line EF is N45° E The bearing of line FG is
    A. S70° E
    B. S75° E
    C. S80° E
    D. S85° E

15. The North Star is named

    A. Polaris   B. Arcturus
    C. Ursa Major   D. Ursa Minor

16. If the bearing of line EF is N30° E, the reverse bearing, Line FE, is

    A. N30° W   B. S60° W   C. S30° E   D. S30° W

17. The diameter of a shaft to be machined is .990" ± .002" The diameter of a shaft that would be unacceptable is, in inches,

    A. .993   B. .992   C. .991   D. .990

18. A lathe is used primarily to machine _____ surfaces.

    A. plane   B. cylindrical
    C. horizontal   D. vertical

19. Brass is an alloy made primarily of

    A. tin and copper   B. tin and lead
    C. tin and zinc   D. copper and zinc

20. A trade name for shatterproof glass is

   A. textron   B. lexon   C. corlon   D. arcon

21. If the sine 10°-40' is 0.18509 and the sine 10°-50' is 0.18795, the sine 10°-46' is most nearly

   A. .18664   B. .18669   C. .18675   D. .18681

22. 8 3/8 inches, in decimals of a foot, is most nearly

   A. .692   B. .695   C. .698   D. .700

23. $(x-1)^3$ is equal to

   A. $x^3 - 3x^2 + 3x - 1$
   B. $x^3 + 3x^2 - 3x - 1$
   C. $x^3 - 2x^2 + 2x - 1$
   D. $x^3 + 2x^2 - 2x - 1$

24. If $Q = AC\sqrt{RS}$, R is equal to

   A. $\dfrac{Q^2}{AC^2S}$ B. $\dfrac{Q^2}{A^2C^2S^2}$ C. $\dfrac{Q^2}{ACS}$ D. $\dfrac{Q^2}{A^2C^2S}$

25. The center of gravity of a triangle is the intersection of its

   A. medians
   B. perpendicular bisectors
   C. angle bisectors
   D. altitudes

KEY (CORRECT ANSWERS)

1.	C	11.	B
2.	C	12.	A
3.	C	13.	B
4.	A	14.	B
5.	D	15.	A
6.	A	16.	D
7.	C	17.	A
8.	A	18.	B
9.	C	19.	D
10.	B	20.	B

21.	D
22.	C
23.	A
24.	D
25.	A

BASIC FUNDAMENTALS OF BLUEPRINT READING

CONTENTS

	Page
CHAPTER 1 - BLUEPRINTS	1
How Prints Are Made	2
Handling Blueprints	2
Folding Blueprints	3
Types of Drawings	3
Charts and Graphs	3
Critical Path Method Diagram	4
Working Drawings	5
CHAPTER 2 - PARTS OF A BLUEPRINT	8
Title Block	8
Revision Block	8
Drawing Number	10
Reference Numbers and Dash Numbers	10
Zone Numbers	10
Scale	10
Station Numbers	11
Material Specifications	11
Heat Treatment	11
Bill of Material	12
Application or Usage Block	14
Finish Marks	14
Notes and Specifications	14
Legends or Symbols	15
Alphabet of Lines	15
Outline Lines	16
Center Lines	16
Hidden Lines	16
Dimension Lines	16
Extension Lines	16
Leaders	16
Cutting Plane Lines	16
Phantom Lines	16
Break Lines	17
Scales	17
Architects' Scale	18
Engineers' Scales	18

Chapter 2 (cont'd)
    Metric Scales — 18
    Graphic Scales — 18

Chapter 3 - READING PROJECTION AND SPECIAL VIEWS — 20
    Orthographic Views — 20
    3-View Drawings — 21
    Questions on the Jig Block — 23
    Pictorial Drawings — 24
      Isometric — 24
      Oblique — 25
      Perspective — 26
    Special Views — 26
    Auxiliary Views — 27
    Rotation — 28
    Phantom Views — 28
    Sections — 28
      Offset Section — 29
      Half Section — 30
      Revolved Section — 30
      Removed Section — 31
      Broken Out Section — 31
      Aligned Section — 31
    Exploded Views — 32
    Developments — 32
    Answer to Questions on Jig Block — 33

BASIC FUNDAMENTALS OF BLUEPRINT READING

CHAPTER 1
BLUEPRINTS

A picture is worth a thousand words. Man has used pictures as a means of communication for many years. It would be almost impossible for an engineer or an inventor to describe the size and shape of a simple object without a drawing of some kind. For example, if an engineer designed a simple object such as the oil filter bracket (Fig. 1-1), it would be difficult to convey his idea to the person who is to fabricate the object without a drawing to show the shape, size, and location of the holes.

Drawing or sketching is the universal language used by engineers, technicians, and skilled craftsmen. Whether this drawing is made freehand or by the use of drawing instruments (mechanical drawing), it is needed to convey all the necessary information to the individual who will fabricate and assemble the object whether it be a building, ship, aircraft, or a mechanical device. If many people are involved in the fabrication of the object, copies will be made of the original drawing or tracing so that all persons involved will have the same information.

Not only are drawings (prints) used as plans to fabricate and assemble objects, they also may be used to illustrate how machines, ships, aircraft, and so on are operated, maintained, repaired, or lubricated.

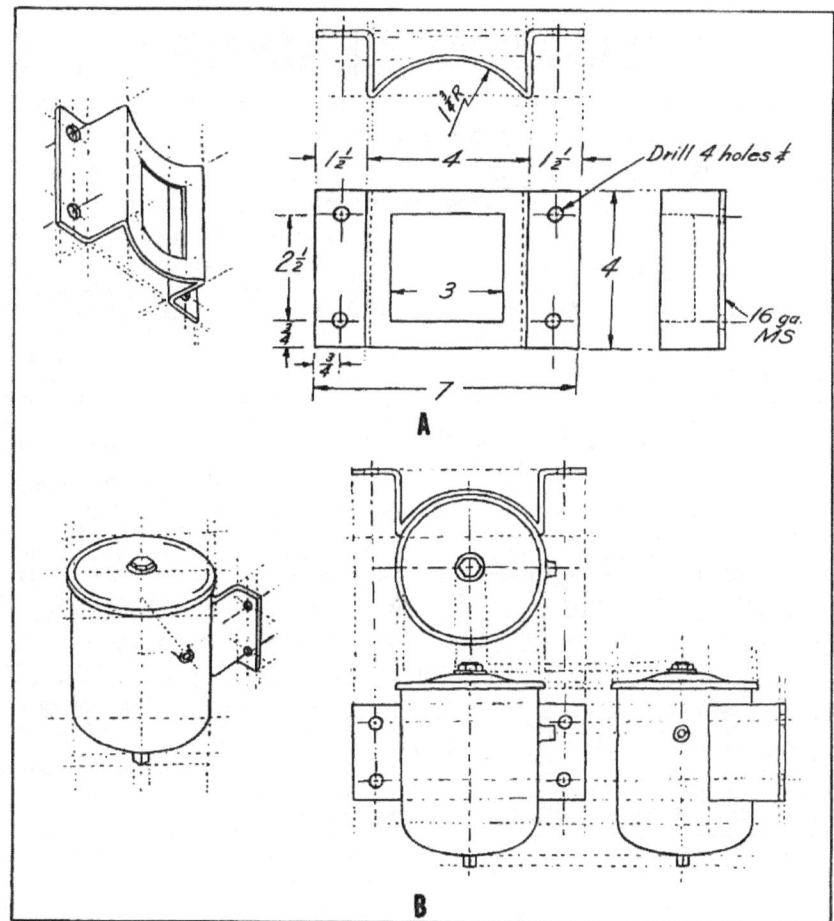

Figure 1-1. A sketch of an oil filter bracket and oil filter assembly.

HOW PRINTS ARE MADE

Blueprints are reproduced copies of mechanical or other types of technical drawings, other than the arts (painting, water coloring, etc.).

A mechanical drawing is drawn with instruments such as compasses, ruling pens, T-squares, triangles, and french curves. Prints are reproduced from original drawings in much the same manner as photographic prints are reproduced from negatives.

The original drawings for prints are made by drawing directly on, or tracing a drawing on a translucent tracing paper or cloth, using black waterproof (india) ink or a special pencil. This original drawing is normally referred to as a tracing (master copy). These copies of the tracings are rarely, if ever, sent to a shop or job site. Instead, reproductions of these tracings are made and distributed to persons or offices where needed. These tracings can be used over and over indefinitely if properly handled and stored.

From these tracings, mentioned in the previous paragraph, blueprints are made. The term blueprint is a rather loosely used term in dealing with reproductions of original drawings. One of the first processes devised to reproduce or duplicate tracings produced white lines on a blue background, hence the term blueprints. Today, however, other methods of reproduction have been developed, and they produce prints of different colors. The colors may be brown, black, gray, or maroon. The differences lie in the types of paper and the developing processes used.

A patented paper identified as "BW" paper produces prints with black lines on a white background.

The ammonia process or "OZALIDS" produces prints with either back, blue, or maroon lines on a white background.

Vandyke paper produces a white line on a dark brown background.

Other processes that may be used to reproduce drawings, usually small drawings or sketches, are the office type duplicating machines such as the mimeograph, ditto machines, and the like. One other type of duplicating process rarely used for reproducing working drawings is the photostatic process. This in reality is a photographic process in which a large camera reduces or enlarges a racing or drawing. The photostat has white lines on a dark background when reproduced directly from a tracing or drawing. If the photostated print is then reproduced, it will have brown lines on a white background. Photostats are generally used by various businesses for incorporating reduced size drawings into reports or records.

HANDLING BLUEPRINTS

Blueprints or prints are valuable permanent records that can be used over and over again if necessary. However, if you are to keep these prints as permanent records, you must handle them with care. Here are a few simple rules to follow to preserve these prints:

1. Keep them out of strong sunlight—they will fade.
2. Don't allow them to get wet or smudged with oil or grease; these ingredients seldom dry out completely, thereby making the prints practically useless.
3. Don't make pencil or crayon notations on a print without proper authority. If you get instructions to mark a print, use an appropriate colored pencil and make the markings a permanent part of the print. Yellow is a good color to use on a print with a blue background (blueprint).
4. Keep prints stowed in their proper place so they can be readily located the next time you want to refer to them.

FOLDING BLUEPRINTS

A standardized, accurate system of filing blueprints is necessary in order to have them readily available when necessary.

Most of the prints that you will handle will be received properly folded. Your main concern will be to refold them correctly. You may, however, have occasion to receive prints that have not been folded at all, or have been folded improperly.

The method of folding prints depends upon the type and size of the filing cabinet, and the location of the identifying marks on the prints. It is preferable to place identifying marks at the top of prints when filing them vertically (upright), and at the bottom right corner, when filing them flat. In some cases, construction prints are stored in rolls.

TYPES OF DRAWINGS

In subsequent chapters, the various types of projections, schematics, and diagrams used in machine, architectural and structural, electrical, electronics, plumbing or piping, and topographical drawings, will be covered in detail.

CHARTS AND GRAPHS

Charts and graphs are primarily used to show organization, for analysis of data, and for presentation of statistics for comparison or prediction. The underlying principle of charts and graphs is to show the subdivisions of a whole and the relationship of its parts to one another.

Another popular type of chart or diagram is the PIE chart. Figure 1-5 indicates the percentage and types of elements that are used to meet the standard specification of ASTM (American Society for Testing Materials) B-21, a specification for brass bars, rods, and shapes. The pie chart shows that the B-21 metal is made of the following elements: zinc, 36.6 percent; copper, 62 percent; tin, 1 percent; lead, .20 percent maximum; iron, .10 percent maximum. Adding up all the elements shown in the pie chart will give you a total of 100 percent.

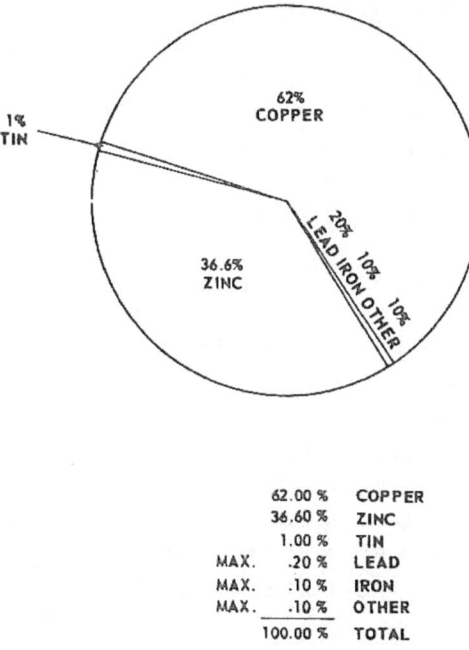

Figure 1-5. Pie Chart.

CRITICAL PATH METHOD DIAGRAM

Another type of graph now in prominent use is the critical path planning method diagram. The critical path method is an outgrowth of the Program Evaluation Review Technique (PERT).

This manual will give you a brief explanation of a simple critical path diagram for constructing a building foundation (footing) (Figure 1-6).

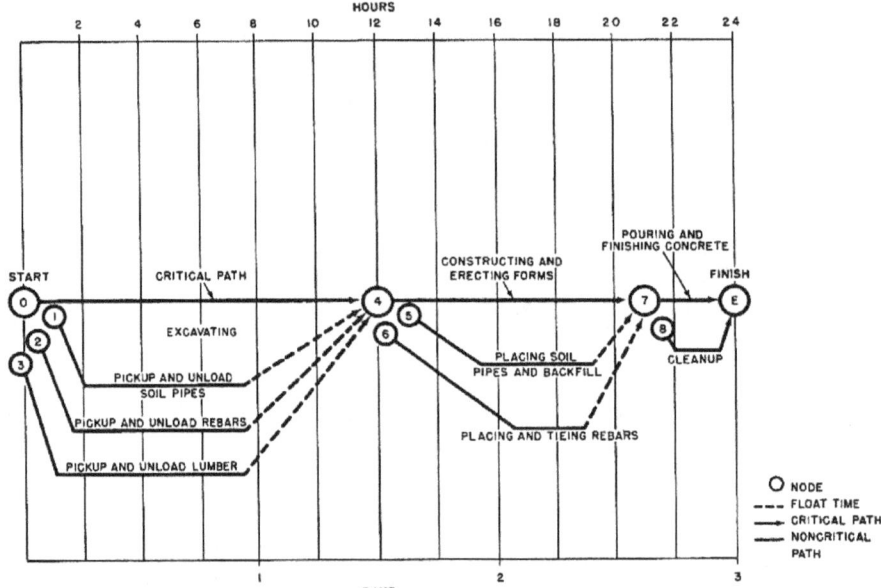

Figure 1-6. Critical path method diagram for constructing a footing.

The critical path is defined as the longest line or path through DEPENDENT SEQUENCES of activities from start to finish. In Figure 1-6, you will note that the critical path is the heavy line preceded by a node and terminated by an arrow (3 are shown). The dependent sequences in this case are: excavating, erecting and building forms, and pouring and finishing the concrete. The forms cannot be built and erected until the excavation is completed; the concrete cannot be poured until the forms and reinforcing bars are in place.

In reading the diagram in Figure 1-6, beginning with node "o," the first phase of the critical path is the excavating. You will note on the diagram that the excavating will be completed in 1½ days (8-hour days). The diagram shows further that, during the period of excavation, the soil pipe, reinforcing bars (rebars), and the lumber can be picked up and delivered to the site in approximately 7 hours; this is shown by the noncritical path lines preceded by nodes 1, 2, and 3. The noncritical path lines are shown on the diagram as being thinner than the critical path line. The dashes (- - - -) at the end of the noncritical path lines indicate float time (free time). In reading this diagram, float time would be approximately 5 hours prior to the completion of the first stage of critical path activity. A critical path line will never indicate float time. The noncritical path activities can be defined as those activities that can be accomplished while another more critical activity is being accomplished.

Node 4 is the beginning of the second sequence of the critical path, and nodes 5 and 6 are the noncritical path of the second sequence, which indicate that while the forms are being built, the soil pipe can be placed and back filled, and the rebars can be placed and tied. The diagram further indicates that noncritical paths 5 and 6 have approximately 2 hours of float time. The third and final sequence along the critical path (node 7) is the pouring and finishing of the concrete footing; the diagram indicates that the project will be completed at the end of the third day. Note that the critical and noncritical sequence (clean-up) are to be completed at the same time, no float time being shown on the noncritical path.

WORKING DRAWINGS

A working drawing is any drawing which is complete enough to give the craftsman all the information needed to fabricate an object. The object referred to may be a bearing for a machine, it may be an aircraft, or a building. A simple object, such as the "guide pin" (Figure 1-7) will require only two views and have all the necessary information on the print. The oil filter bracket, shown earlier in Figure 1-1, required 3 views including an assembly sketch to show the competed object and the position of the parts.

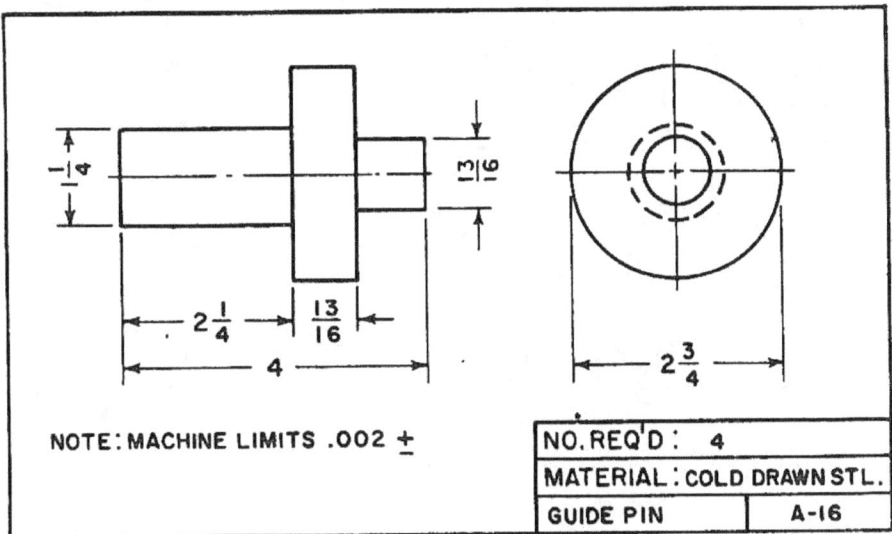

Figure 1-7. A simple working drawing (machine).

In architectural prints, a full set of views is furnished to give the craftsmen all the information required to construct the building. Figure 1-8 shows all views necessary for the craftsmen to build the building, including a detail of the cornice and the foundation.

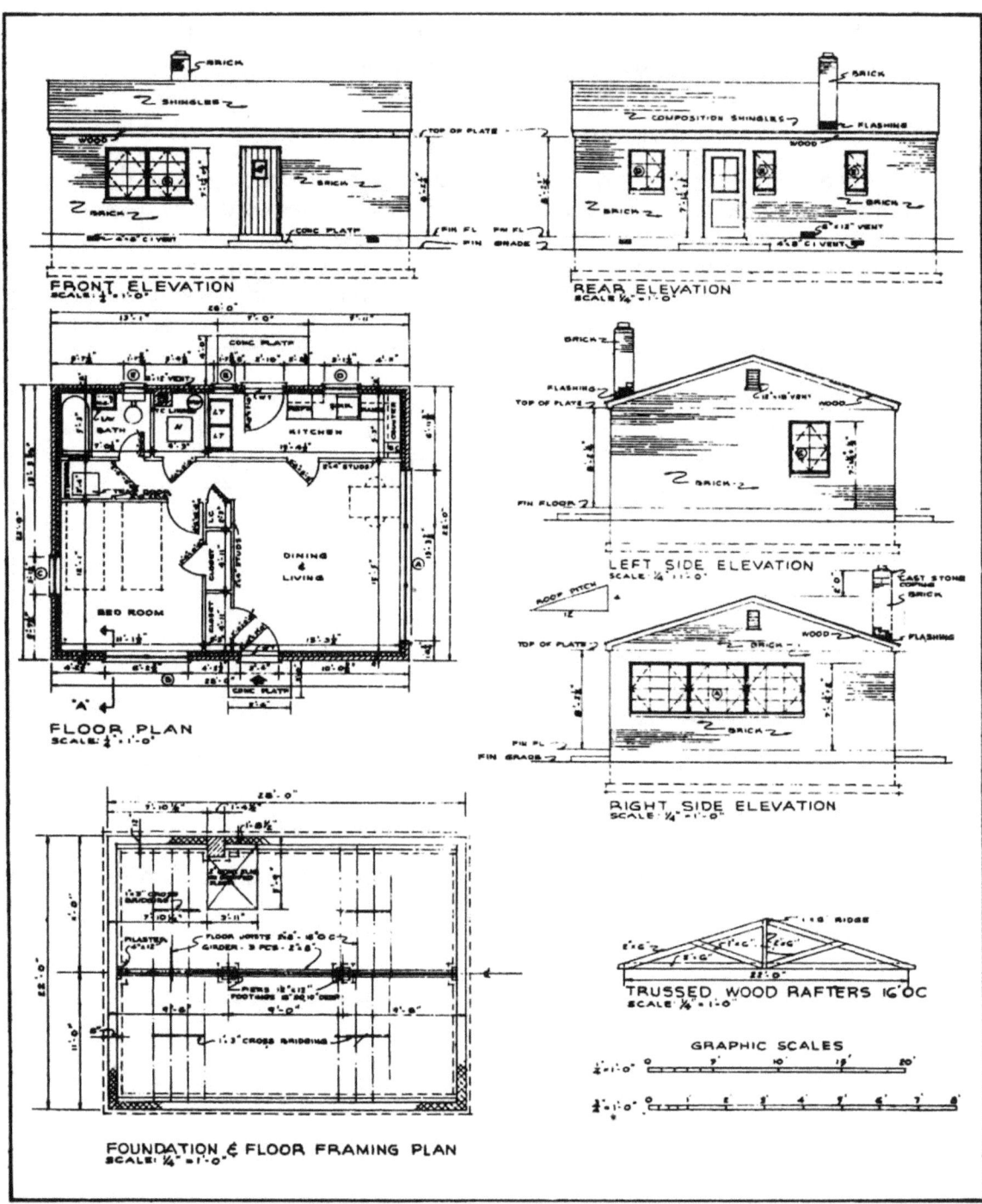

Figure 1-8. A set of architectural prints.

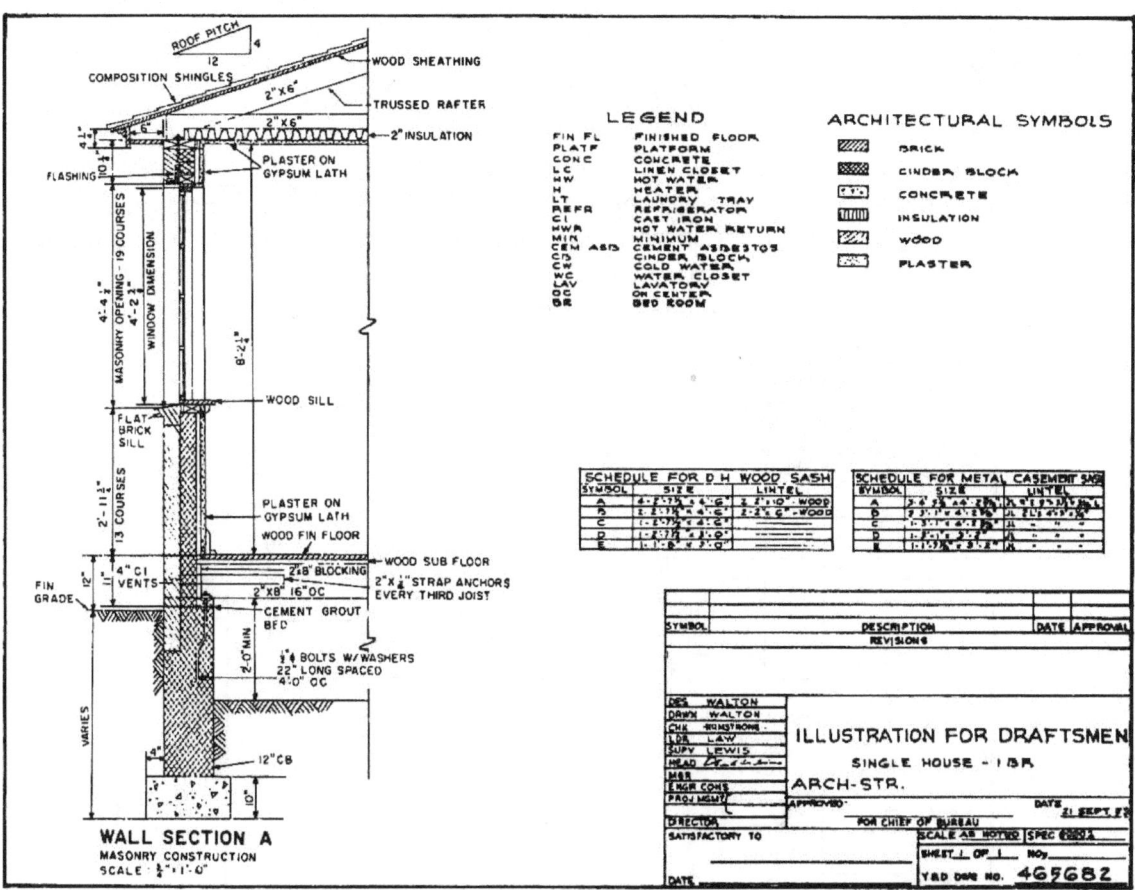

Figure 1-8. A set of architectural prints (continued).

Figure 1-9 shows the types of working drawings required to construct an aircraft. The assembling of an aircraft, in this case, begins with a detail print of the aileron rib; the figure also indicates that the set of prints may contain other details. Then, there is a subassembly print that shows how the aileron rib joins the other parts of the aileron assembly. Next is a unit assembly print, which shows you where the aileron joins the other parts of the wing assembly. The final assembly print shows the entire wing assembly in relation to the completed aircraft.

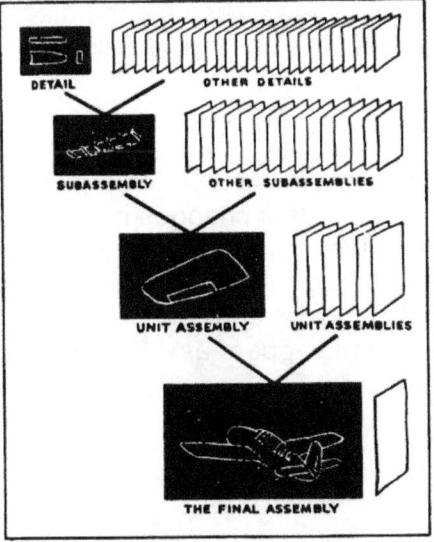

Figure 1-9. Every part, every assembly has its descriptive print.

CHAPTER 2
PARTS OF A BLUEPRINT

The name of the object on the blueprint is given in the title block (Figures 2-1 and 2-2), which is located in the lower right corner of all drawings prepared. Figure 2-1 is the type of title block used in Yards and Docks construction drawings. Figure 2-2 is the type used by BuShips for technical drawings. The title block may appear elsewhere on other blueprints, but the lower right corner is the usual place.

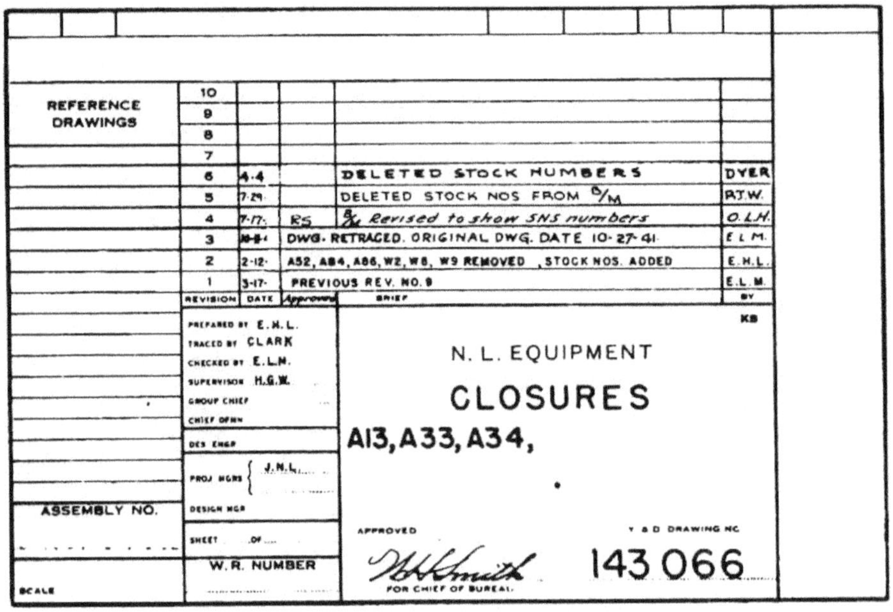

Figure 2-1. Title block (Yards & Docks).

TITLE BLOCK

The title block contains the drawing number and all the information required to identify the part or assembly that the blueprint represents. If a space within the title block has a diagonal or slant line drawn across it, disregard that space, because the diagonal line indicates that the information usually placed in it is not required, or is given elsewhere on the drawing.

REVISION BLOCK

Each drawing shows a revision block located on the right side of the print. Modern practice is to put this space for the recording of changes in the upper right corner, but it may appear above the title. All changes to the drawing are noted in this block and are dated and identified by a number or a letter. If, for some reason, a revision block is not used, a revised drawing may be shown by the addition of a letter to the original number; for example, if the print shown in Figure 2-1 were revised, it would appear as 143066-A.

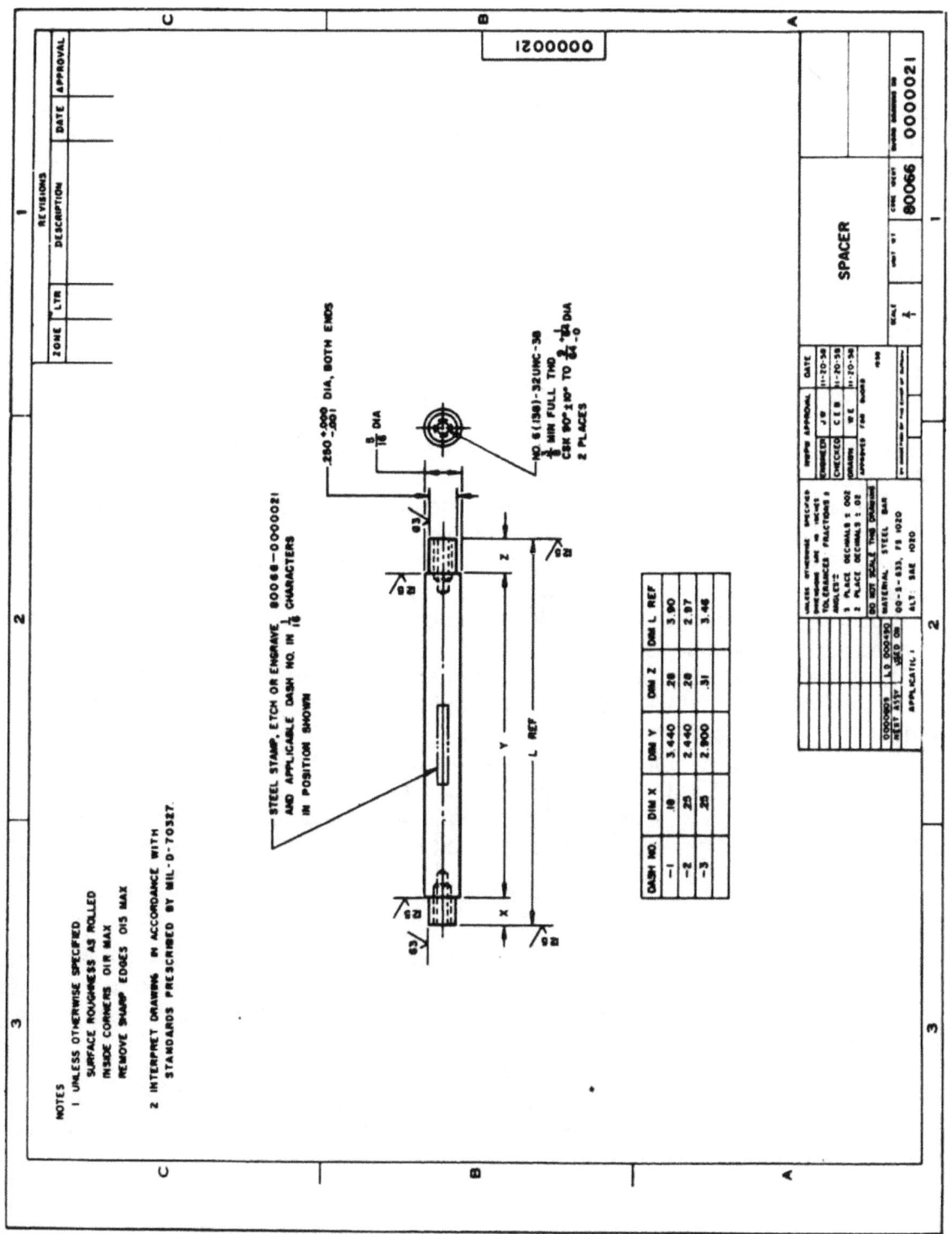

Figure 2-2. Format of a BuWeps drawing sheet.

DRAWING NUMBER

All drawings are identified by a drawing number, which appears in a number block in the lower right corner of the title block. It may be shown in other places also; for example, near the top border line, in the upper corner, or on the reverse side at both ends so that it will be visible when a drawing is rolled up. Its purpose is to permit quick identification of a blueprint number. If a blueprint has more than one sheet, and each sheet has the same number, this information is included in the number block indicating the sheet number and the number of sheets in the series. For example, note that in the title block shown in Figure 2-1, the sheet is page 2 of 8 sheets.

REERENCE NUMBERS AND DASH NUMBERS

Reference numbers that appear in the title block refer to numbers of other blueprints. When more than one detail is shown on a drawing, dash and numbers are frequently used. For example, if two parts are shown in one detail drawing, both prints would have the same drawing number, plus a dash and an individual number, such as 8117041-1 and 8117041-2.

In addition to appearing in the title block, the dash and numbers may appear on the face of the drawings near the parts they identify. Some commercial prints show the drawing and dash numbers and point with a leader line to the part; others use a circle, 3/8 inch in diameter, around the dash number, and carry a leader line to the part.

A dash and numbers are used to identify modified or improved parts, and also to identify right-hand and left-hand parts.

Many aircraft parts on the left-hand side of an aircraft are exactly like the corresponding parts on the right-hand side—in reverse. The left-hand part is always shown in the drawing. The right-hand part is called for in the title block.

Above the title block you will see a notation, such as "159674 LH shown; 159674-1 RH opposite. Both parts carry the same number. But the part called for is distinguished by a dash and number. LH means left-hand, and RH means right-hand. Some companies use odd numbers for right-hand and even numbers for left-hand parts.

ZONE NUMBERS

Zone numbers on blueprints serve the same purpose as the numbers and letters printed on borders of maps to help you locate a particular point. To find a point, you mentally draw horizontal and vertical lines from these letters and numerals, and the point where these lines intersect is the area sought.

You will use practically the same system to help you locate parts, sections, and views on large blueprinted objects (for example, assembly drawings of aircraft). Parts numbered in the title block can be located on the drawing by looking up the numbers in squares along the lower border. Zone numbers read from right to left.

SCALE

The scale of the blueprint is indicated in one of the spaces within the title block. It indicates the size of the drawing as compared with the actual size of the part. The scale is usually shown as 1" = 2" = 12", ½" = 1", and so on. It may also be indicat4ed as full size, one-half size, one-fourth size, and so on.

If a blueprint indicates that the scale is 1" = 2", each line on the print is shown one-half its actual length. A scale showing 3" = 1", each line on the print is three times its actual length.

Very small parts are enlarged to show the views clearly, and large objects are normally reduced in size to fit on a standard size drawing paper. In short, the scale is selected to fit the object being drawn and space available on a sheet of drawing paper.

Remember: NEVER MEASURE A DRAWING. USE DIMENSIONS. Why? Because the print may have been reduced in size from the original drawing; reduction errors may have been introduced which you would include by a physical measurement. Or, you might not take the scale of the drawing into consideration. Then, too, paper stretches and shrinks as the humidity changes, thus introducing perhaps the greatest source of error in actually taking a measurement by laying a rule on the print itself. Play it safe and READ the dimensions on the drawing; they always remain the same.

Graphical scales are often placed on maps and plot plans. These scales indicate the number or feet or miles represented by an inch. A fraction is often used, as 1/500, meaning that one unit on the map is equal to 500 like units on the ground. A LARGE-SCALE MAP has a scale of 1" = 10'; a map with a scale of 1" = 1000' is considered to be a SMALL-SCALE MAP.

STATION NUMBERS

On large assemblies—aircrafts, for example—a numbering system is used to help locate STATIONS on the aircraft assembly, such as the fuselage frame shown in Figure 2-3. When you see "Fuselage Frames-Sta. 90.00," you know that the frame is 90 inches aft the nose. The reference datum is usually taken from the nose or zero station of the aircraft; sometimes, however, it is taken from the firewall.

The same station system is used for wing and stabilizer frames. The measurement is taken from the center line, or zero station, of the aircraft. Station numbers for a typical aircraft are shown in Figure 2-3.

MATERIAL SPECIFICATIONS

When working from prints, you should ALWAYS USE THE MATERIAL SPECIFIED. NEVER make a substitution unless you have the proper authorization. The material indicated was selected by an engineer because it meets the requirements of the job. It is the best material for that particular part. Only an engineer or a person having the authority of an engineer for a particular piece of work can authorize substitutions of material when the kind specified is not available.

HEAT TREATMENT

Practically all metals require some form of heat treatment in a manufacturing process. The title block on a blueprint, drawing, or specification lists the type of heat treatment required. Frequently it is necessary to remove the temper from a piece of metal, in order that it may be machined to specifications, after which it must be retempered or hardened. Reference should be made to the heat treatment specifications in the title block to determine the type required and the point during processing at which heat treatment is to occur.

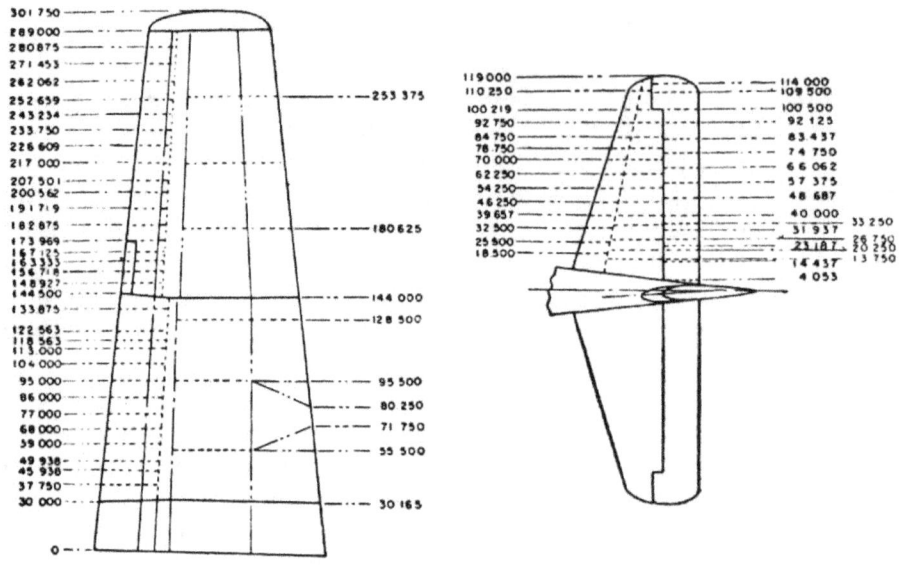

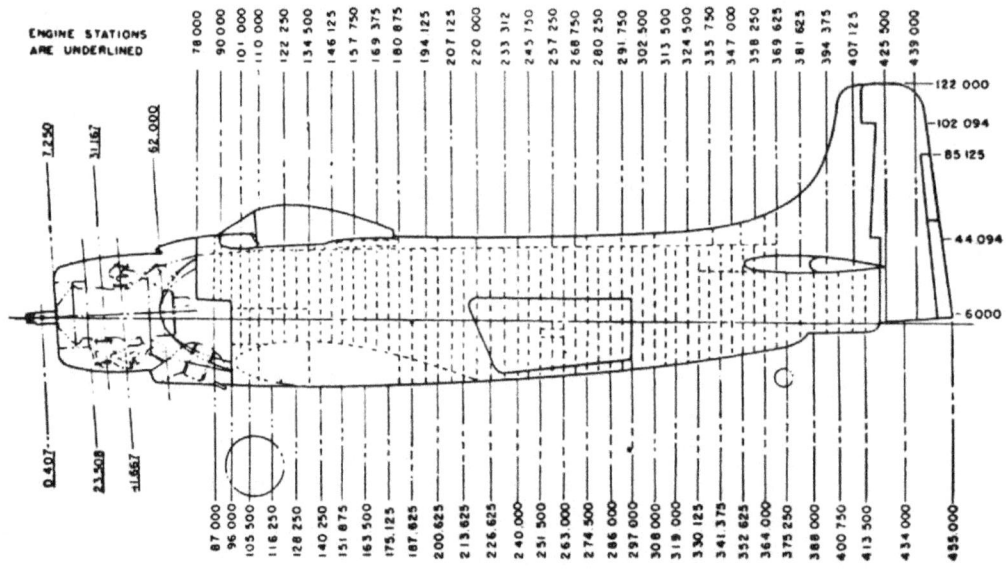

Figure 2-3. Aircraft stations and frames.

BILL OF MATERIAL

A special block or box on the drawing may contain a list of the pieces of stock necessary to make a part of an assembly of several parts. It is called a BILL OF MATERIAL or SCHEDLE (Figure 2-4) and indicates the type of stock, the size and the specific amount required.

The bill of material often contains a list of standard parts, known as a parts list or schedule. Many commonly used items, such as machine bolts, screws, turnbuckles, rivets, pipefittings, valves, and so on, have been standardized.

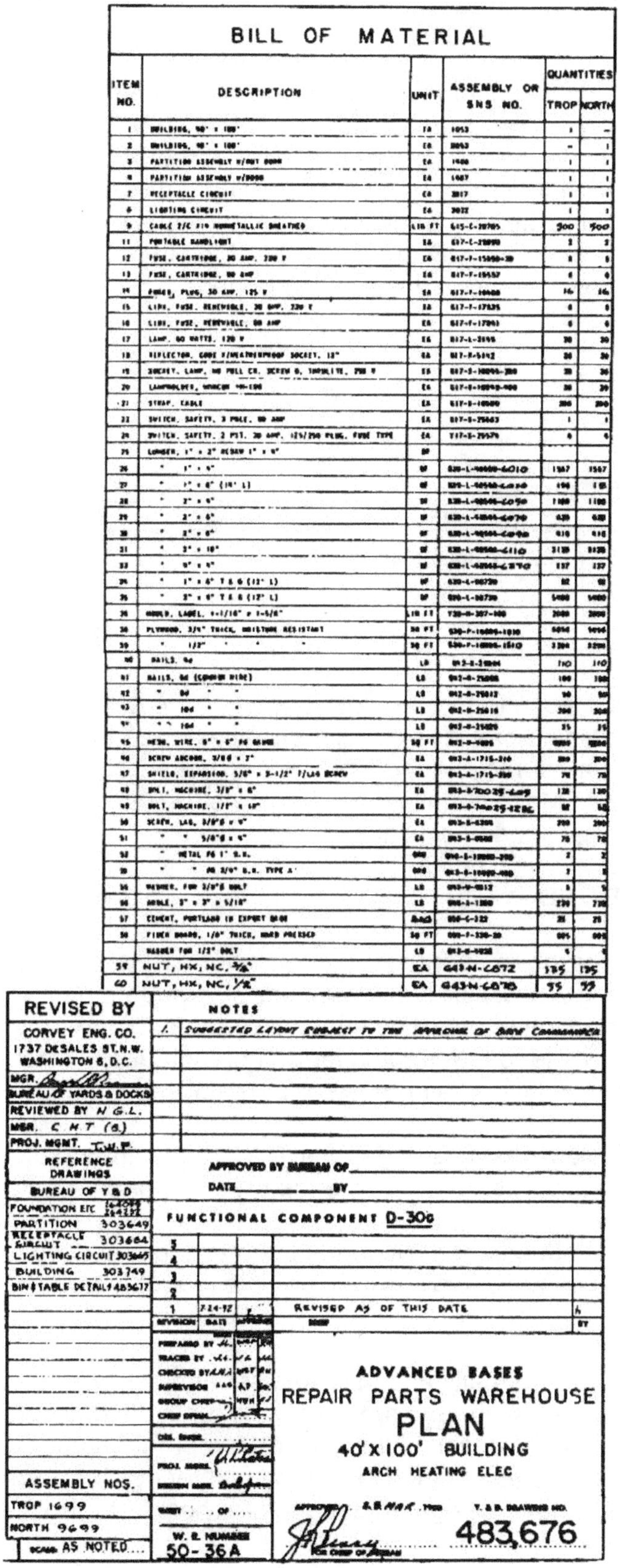

Figure 2-4. A bill of material (schedule).

APPLICATION OR USAGE BLOCK

A usage block may be used to identify, by their drawing numbers, the larger units of which the detail part of subassembly shown on the drawing forms a component. This block is usually located near the title block, or it may form a part of the list of the bill of material. The general purpose of the USAGE or APPLICATION block is to provide a means for determining the equipment in which the part or assembly shown on the drawing is used. This block reveals the parts and assemblies that have a diversity of uses, and it aids in determining the effects of a change in the part or assembly shown on the drawing (Figure 2-5). See also Figure 2-1.

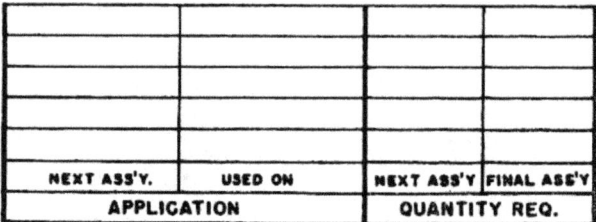

Figure 2-5. Application or usage blocks.

FINISH MARKS

Finish marks (✓) illustrated in Figure 2-2) are used to indicate surfaces that must be finished by machining. Machining provides a better surface appearance and provides the fit with closely mated parts. In manufacturing, during the finishing process, the required limits and tolerances must be observed. Machined finishes should not be confused with finishes of paint, enamel, grease, chromium plating, and similar coating.

NOTES AND SPECIFICATIONS

Blueprints contain all the information about an objector part which can be presented graphically (that is, in drawing). A considerable amount of information can be presented this way, but there is more information required by supervisors, contractors, manufacturers, and craftsmen, which is not adaptable to the graphic form of presentation. Information of this type is generally given on the drawings as notes or as a set of specifications attached to the drawings.

NOTES are generally placed on drawings to give additional information to clarify the object on the blueprint. Leader lines are used to indicate the precise part being notated.

A SPECIFICATION is a statement or document containing a description or enumeration of particulars, as the terms of a contract, or details of an object or objects not shown on a blueprint or drawing.

Specifications (specs) are normally attached to a set of blueprints to: describe items so that they may be procured, assembled, and maintained to function in accordance with the performance requirements; furnish sufficient information to permit determination of conformance to the description; and furnish the above in sufficient completeness for accomplishment without the need of research, development, design engineering, or help from the preparing organization.

LEGENDS OR SYMBOLS

The legend is generally placed in the upper right corner of a blueprint, if space permits. The legend is used to explain or define a symbol or special mark placed on a blueprint. Figure 2-6 shows a legend for an electrical plan of a building.

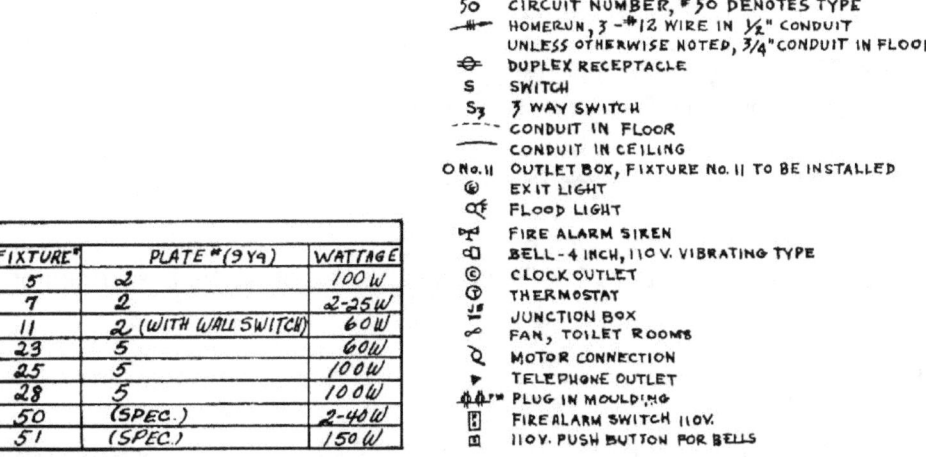

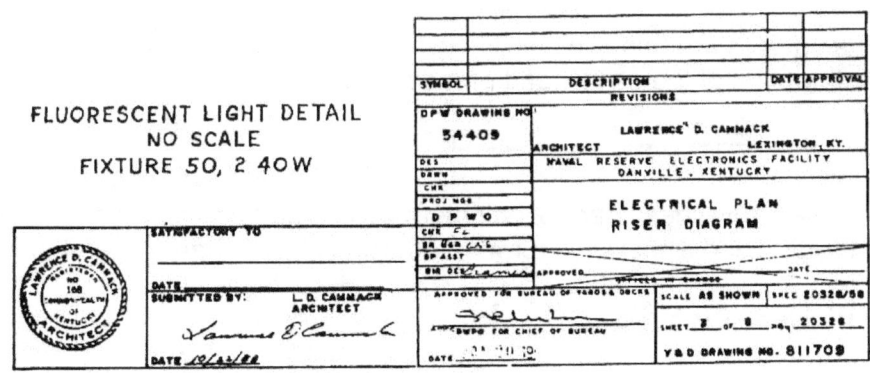

Figure 2-6. An electrical plan (note the legend).

ALPHABET OF LINES

In order to be able to read blueprints, you must acquire a knowledge of the use of lines. The alphabet of lines is the common language of the technician and the engineer. Just as a word in the spoken language requires letters of the alphabet to have meaning, the object on the blueprint requires several different types of lines in order to impart information to the reader of the blueprint.

OUTLINE LINES ─────────────

The outline lines are thick solid lines that represent the edges and surfaces that are visible from the angle at which the original drawing was made.

CENTER LINES ───── ── ───── ── ─────

The center lines are thin lines composed of long and short dashes, alternately and evenly spaced with a long dash at each end. The center lines signify the center of a circle or arc, and are also used to divide drawings into equal or symmetrical parts. Center lines are always used to locate the center of any hollowed part of an object.

HIDDEN LINES ── ── ── ── ── ── ── ── ── ──

Hidden lines are medium lines which consist of short dashes evenly spaced. They show the hidden features of a part. Figure 2-7 illustrates the use of all the lines mentioned in this chapter.

DIMENSION LINES ◄─────   ─────►

Dimension lines are thin lines which indicate the size of objects on a blueprint. There are two methods of showing dimensions on a blueprint; one is by reading the dimension that is placed in the break of the dimension line, and the other is a dimension line without a break terminated by arrows, with the dimension shown above the line. In either case, the dimension distance is read from the point of one arrowhead to the point of the other arrowhead.

EXTENSION LINES ─────────────

Extension lines are thin lines which indicate the extent of a dimension and will always be touched by the point of the arrowhead of a dimension line.

LEADERS ◄─────────────

Leaders are thin lines used to indicate a part or portion to which a number, note, or other information refers, and are always terminated with an arrowhead. See Figure 2-7.

CUTTING PLANE LINES ▼────·····────▼

A cutting plane is a thick line which indicates the path of the object that is cut to show a section. Referring to Figure 2-7, you will note that the cutting plane line has the arrowheads pointing to the left. The section view to the right (Section A-A) is to be viewed looking in the direction in which the arrowheads are pointing.

PHANTOM LINES ───── ── ── ───── ──

Phantom lines are medium lines used to indicate the alternate position of parts of the item delineated, repeated detail, or the relative position of an absent part. In Figure 2-7, the phantom lines are used to show the relative position of an absent part.

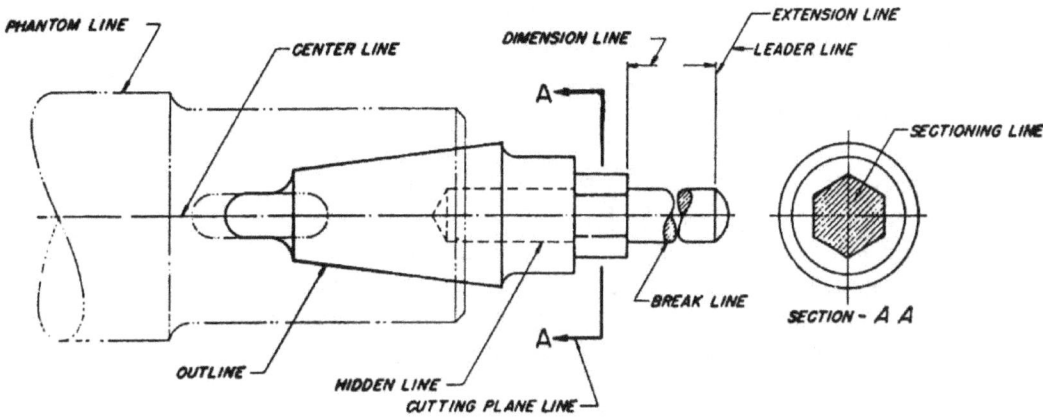

Figure 2-7. Line conventions

BREAK LINES

The LONG BREAK LINE simply indicates that a part or object has been shortened. It is merely a space saver for the draftsman; it does not change the actual length indicated by the dimension.

The SHORT BREAK LINE indicates that the draftsman has removed part of an outer surface to reveal the inside structure.

Break lines used to shorten metal rods, metal tubes, metal bars, and wood, are shown in Figure 2-8; also shown are the long and short break lines.

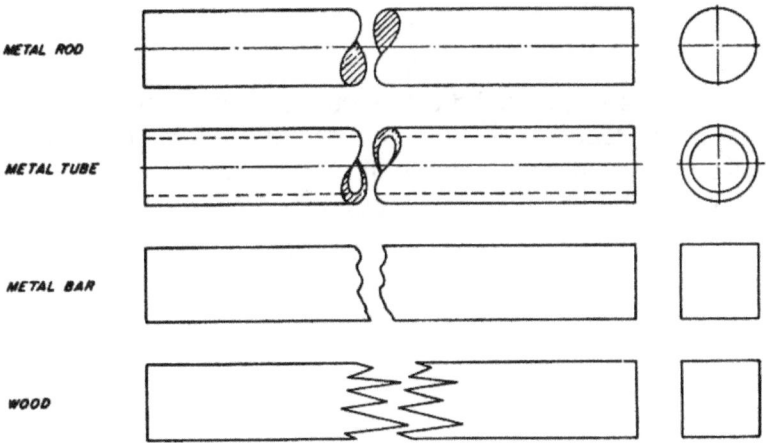

Figure 2-8. Break lines.

SCALES

Any graduated instrument or measuring stick used to measure distance or length may be called a scale, but technically the graduations themselves are the scale. Scales are made in a wide variety of shapes, sizes, and materials, and for many purposes.

Because the space of a drawing sheet does not permit objects to be shown in their actual dimensions (true size), dimensions in accurate proportion to actual dimensions of the objects are used. Large objects must be drawn to a reduced size or very small objects must be drawn to an enlarged size. The scale provides the draftsman with an instrument which enables him to lay out on the drawing proportional dimensions quickly and easily.

ARCHITECTS' SCALE

Architects' Scales (Figure 2-9) are divided into proportional feet and inches and are generally used in scaling drawings for machine and structural work. The triangular architects' scale usually contains 11 scales, each subdivided differently. Six scales read from the left end, while five scales read from the right end. Figure 2-9 shows how the 3/16-inch subdivision of the architects' scale is further subdivided into 12 equal parts representing 1 inch each, and the 3/32-inch subdivision into 6 equal parts representing 2 inches each.

ENGINEERS' SCALES

Engineers' Scales (Figure 2-9) are divided into decimal graduations (10, 20, 30, 40, 50, and 60 divisions to the inch). These scales are used for plotting and map drawing and in the graphic solution of problems.

METRIC SCALES

Metric Scales (Figure 2-9) are used in conjunction with drawings, maps, and so forth, made in countries using the metric system. This system is also being used with increasing frequency in the United States. The scale is divided into centimeters and millimeters. In conversion, 2.54 cm (centimeters) are equal to 1 inch.

GRAPHIC SCALES

Graphic Scales (Figure 2-9) are lines subdivided into distances corresponding to convenient units of length on the ground or of the object represented by the blueprint. They are placed in or near the title block of the drawing and their relative lengths to the scales of the drawing are not affected if the print is reduced or enlarged.

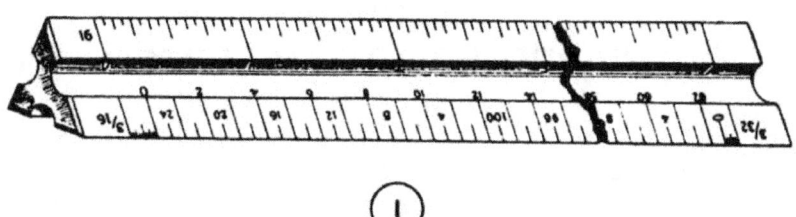

①

ARCHITECTS' SCALE

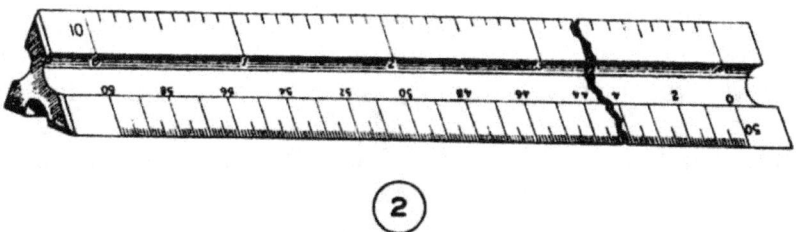

②

ENGINEERS' SCALE

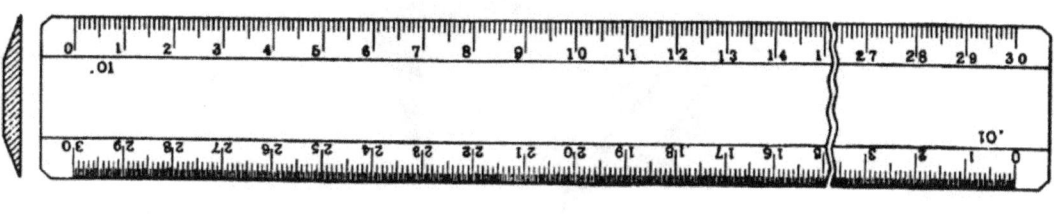

③

METRIC SCALE

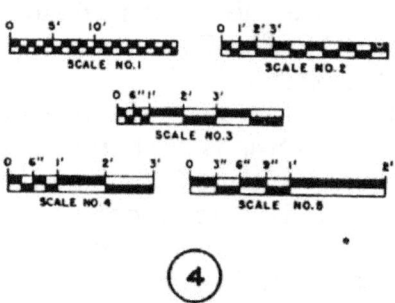

④

GRAPHIC SCALES

Figure 2-9. Types of scales.

CHAPTER 3
READING PROJECTION AND SPECIAL VIEWS

In learning to read blueprints, you must develop the ability to visualize the object (Figure 3-1) by properly interpreting the various types of lines, dimensions, sections, details, symbols, views, and other media used by the designer or draftsman in drawing an object or parts of an object to be utilized by a craftsman or engineer.

You probably did some visualizing when you planned your last long road trip. You consulted a road map to find the best roads to your destination, the approximate distance, the direction, and so on. These were indicated on the map by various widths and colors of lines and symbols. You did not actually see the roads, you knew by checking the colors and symbols that the relatively wide red lines were primary roads. Two red lines side by side were dual highways, dark blue lines were secondary roads, light blue lines were creeks, sky blue areas were marked as lakes and rivers, and so on. Basically, the same techniques used to read a road map can be applied to reading a blueprint.

Figure 3-1. Visualizing a blueprint.

ORTHOGRAPHIC VIEWS

Prints that furnish complete information for construction and repair present an object in its true proportions. These prints are accurate and indicate true shape and size. These prints are usually drawn by ORTHOGRAPHIC PROJECTION, a parallel projection in which the projectors are perpendicular to the plane of projection.

The number of views to be used in projecting a drawing is governed by the complexity of the shape of the drawing. Complex drawings are normally drawn showing six views; that is, both ends, front, top, rear, and bottom (Figure 3-2). Figure 3-2 shows an object placed in a transparent box hinged at the edges. The projections on the sides of the box are the views seen by looking straight at the object through each side. If the outlines are scribed on each surface and the box opened as shown and laid flat, the result is a 6-view, orthographic projection drawing. It should be noted, also, that the rear plane may be considered hinged to either of the side planes or to the top or bottom plane; thus, the rear view may be shown in any one of four positions (to the right of the right side view or left of the left side view, above the top view or below the bottom view). As a general rule, you will find that most drawings will be presented in three views. Occasionally, you will see 2-view drawings, particularly cylindrical objects.

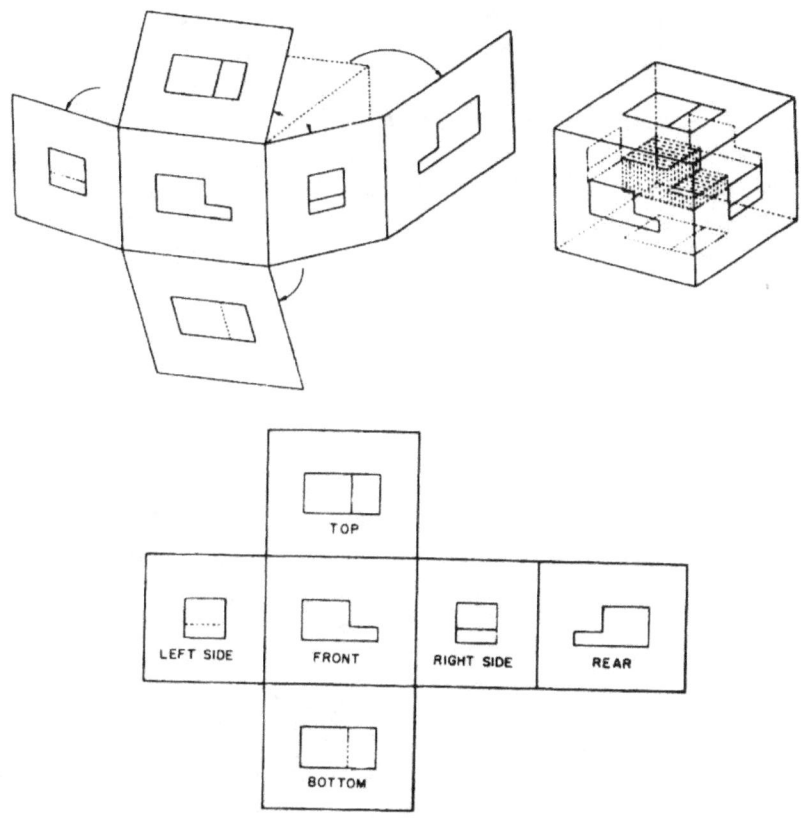

Figure 3-2. Third-angle orthographic projection.

3-VIEW DRAWINGS

A 3-view orthographic projection drawing generally shows the FRONT, TOP, AND RIGHT SIDE view of an object. Refer back to Figure 3-2 and note the position of the front, top, and right side view; by eliminating the rear, bottom, and left side view, the drawing is changed from a 6-view drawing to a conventional 3-view drawing.

Study the arrangement of the three views shown in Figure 3-3. The front view is the starting point. It was selected as the front view because it shows the most characteristic feature of the object—the notch.

The right side or end view is projected to the right of the front view. Note that all the horizontal outlines of the front view are extended horizontally to make up the side view. After you study each view of the object, you should be able to visualize the object as it appears in Figure 3-4. In order to clarify the 3-view drawing further, think of the object as being immovable (Figure 3-5), and that you are moving around it. This will help you to relate the blueprint views to the appearance of the object concerned.

In summarizing the visualization of the object shown in Figures 3-3, 3-4, and 3-5, you should have obtained the following knowledge about the object: the shape of the object, the overall length of the object which is $2\frac{1}{8}$ inches. The object is $1\frac{3}{8}$ inches high, and $\frac{7}{8}$ inch from the bottom.

To take you one step further, study the 3-view drawing illustrated in Figure 3-6. Note that in this illustration the shape of the object is similar to that shown in Figure 3-3, with one exception; the object in Figure 3-6 has a ½-inch hole drilled in the notched portion of the object.

22

This drawing is read in the same manner as the other 3-view drawing. The hidden lines shown on the front view of the drawing tell you the exact location of the walls of this hole (½ inch). The hidden lines are also shown on the side view. You must remember, in viewing this object from the front, the drilled hole is not visible; that is the reason for the hidden lines. This is also true in looking from the right side.

The 3-view drawing shown in Figure 3-6 introduces two more symbols from the "alphabet of lines" that are not shown in Figure 3-3: the hidden line, and the center line which gives the location of the exact center of the drilled hole. The shape and size of the object are the same.

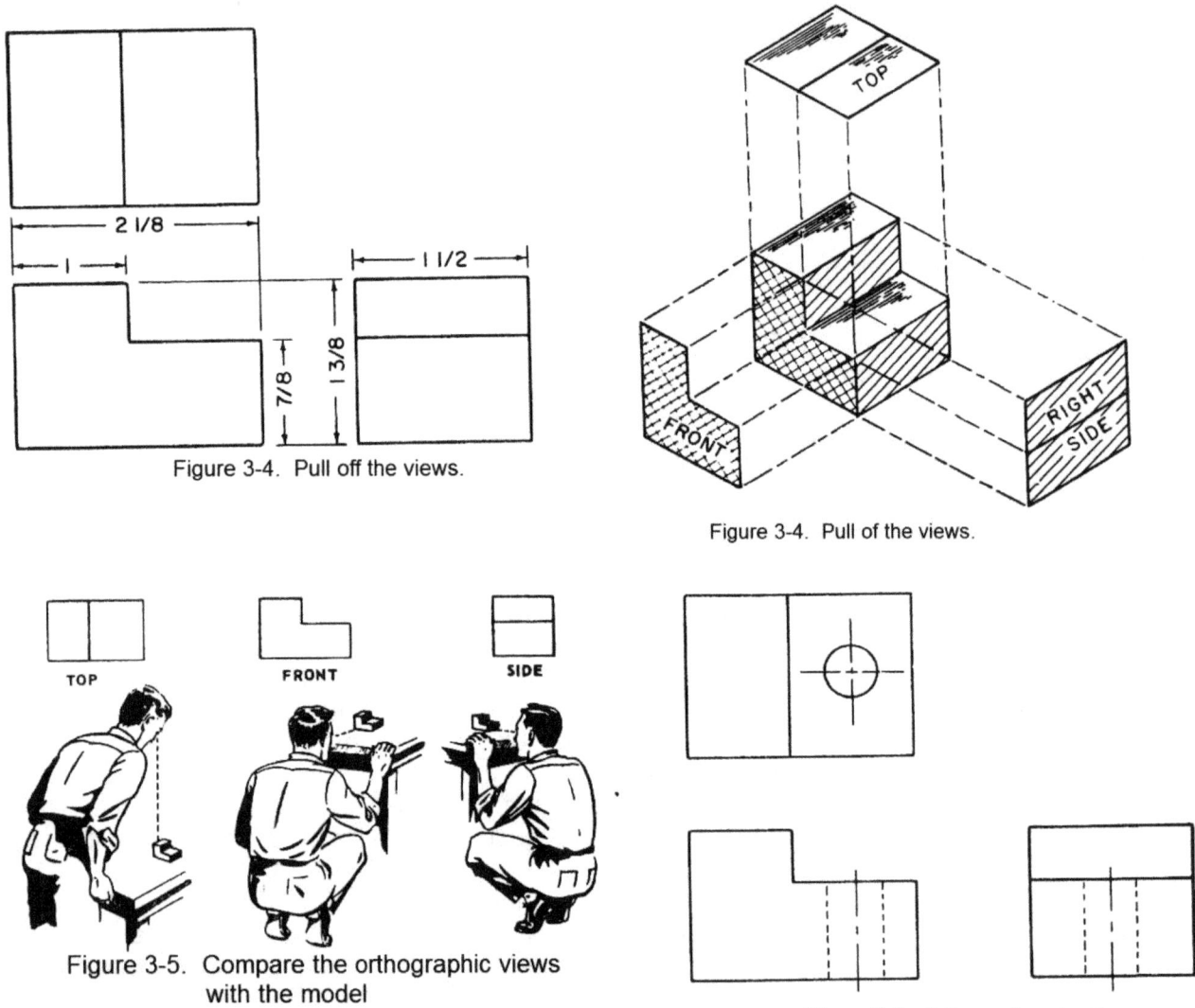

Figure 3-4. Pull off the views.

Figure 3-4. Pull of the views.

Figure 3-5. Compare the orthographic views with the model

Figure 3-6. A three-view drawing.

As a test of your ability to visualize and interpret simple 3-view drawings, answer the following questions pertaining to Figure 3-7. The answers are given at the end of this chapter.

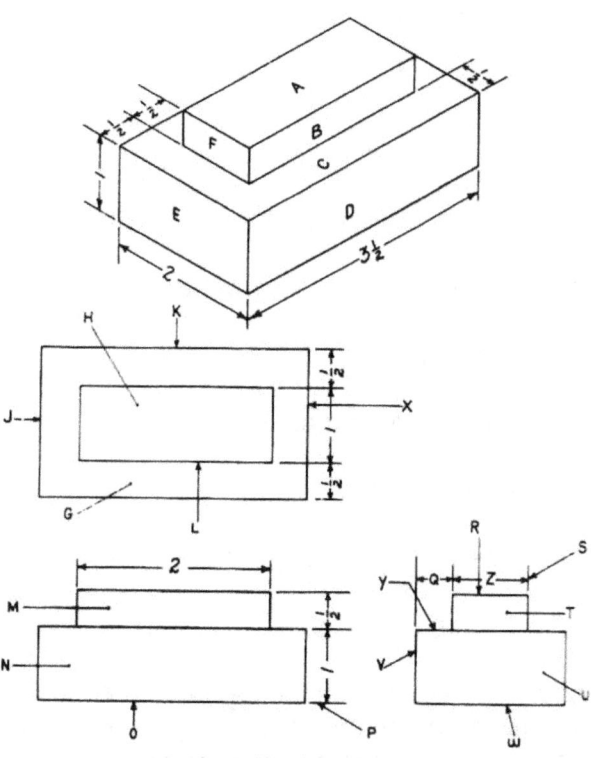

Figure 3-7. Jig block.

1. What is the overall height of the jig block? 1._____

2. What is the overall width of the jig block? 2._____

3. What is the overall length of the jig block? 3._____

4. What surface in the top view represents A? 4._____

5. What kind of lines are J, O, W, X, Y, and V? 5._____

6. Surface D is represented by what letter in the front view? 6._____

7. F is represented by what letter in the side view? 7._____

8. What is the dimension of Z? 8._____

9. What is the dimension of Q? 9._____

10. What type of lines are Q and Z? 10._____

11. What kind of lines are P and S? 11._____

12. Surface B is represented by what surface in the front view? 12._____

13. Surface C is represented by what surface in the top view? 13.____

14. What is the width of surface H? 14.____

15. What is the length of surface M? 15.____

16. Surface E is represented by what surface on the side view? 16.____

17. Surface B is represented by what letter in the top view? 17.____

18. How many jig blocks are to be made? 18.____

19. What type of metal is the jig block to be made of? 19.____

20. What letter or letters denote(s) extension line(s)? 20.____

21. What letters in the top view denote outlines or visible lines? 21.____

PICTORIAL DRAWINGS

The purpose of a pictorial drawing is to show general location, function, and appearance of parts and assemblies. There are three common types of pictorial views drawn by draftsmen: (1) the isometric, (2) the oblique (cavalier and cabinet), and (3) the perspective.

ISOMETRIC

The isometric drawing is the most commonly used and the most useful in making freehand sketches.

In an isometric drawing, all lines that are parallel on the object are also parallel on the drawing. Vertical lines are shown in a vertical position, but lines representing horizontal lines are drawn at an angle of 30° with the horizontal. Also, on an isometric drawing, all the lines which represent the horizontal and vertical lines on an object have true length. Since all isometric lines are spread equally (120°)—the same scale of measure is used on the 3 visible sides. Isometric drawings (Figure 3-8) may be dimensioned, and blueprints of these drawings may be used for making simple objects. But, isometric drawings cannot be used alone for complicated parts or structures. Isometric drawings may be used as an aid in clarifying the orthographic drawings that are the foundation of all construction blueprints.

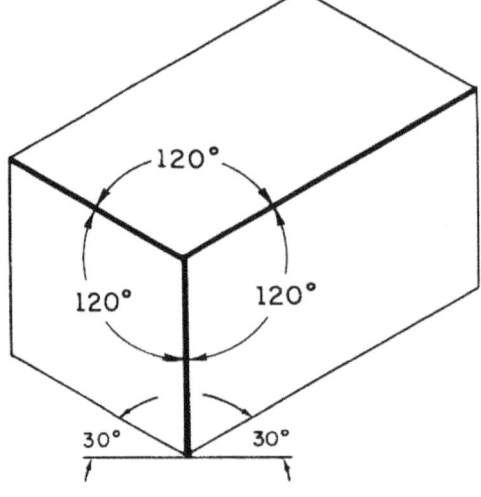

Figure 3-8. Isometric drawing.

OBLIQUE

In an oblique drawing, the front face of the object is shown in its true size and shape as if it were an orthographic (6- or 3-view) drawing, and the receding lines of the other two sides shown are drawn obliquely at any angle, usually 30°, 45°, or 60° to the horizontal (Figure 3-9). Measuring scale for the oblique sides may be any selected scale to give the object realistic depth (normally ¾ the scale of the front view).

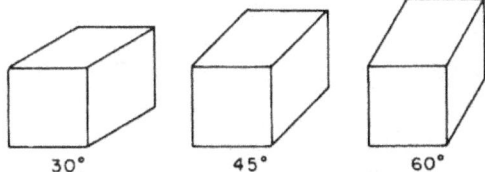

Figure 3-9. Oblique views of a rectangular block.

CABINET DRAWING (Figure 3-10) is an oblique drawing with a special name because it is often used for drawings of cabinet work. It is distinguished by the use of ½ scale measurements on the oblique sides, compared to full scale measurements on the front plane. Cabinet drawings are commonly drawn with the oblique sides at 30° or 45°.

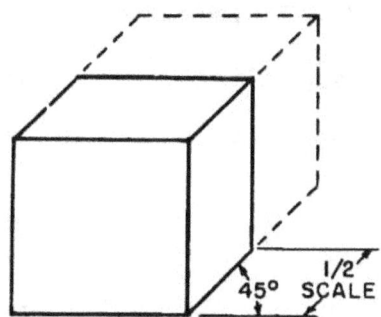

Figure 3-10. A cabinet drawing of a cube.

A CAVALIER DRAWING (Figure 3-11) is another special type of oblique projection wherein the receding or oblique planes are drawn to the same scale as that used on the front plane. This creates a drawing distorted from the object's true proportions, but allows the use of one scale of measure for the entire drawing. Cavalier drawings are drawn with the oblique planes 45° to the front plane.

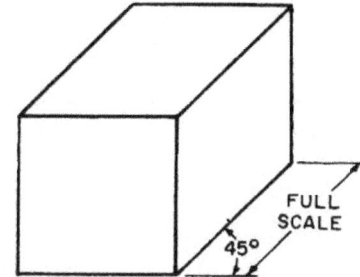

Figure 3-11. A cavalier drawing of a cube.

PERSPECTIVE

The most truly pictorial method of presentation is perspective drawing. By this method, objects are made to appear proportionately smaller with distance just as they do when you look at them (Figure 3-12). However, perspective drawings are difficult to draw and, since lines on perspective drawings are drawn in diminishing proportion to the edges represented, a perspective drawing cannot be used when an object is to be constructed. It is of value chiefly for illustrative purposes, particularly for technical illustration in the commercial and architectural fields.

Figured 3-12. The perspective.

Note the differences among the isometric oblique, the cavalier, and the cabinet drawing shown in Figure 3-13.

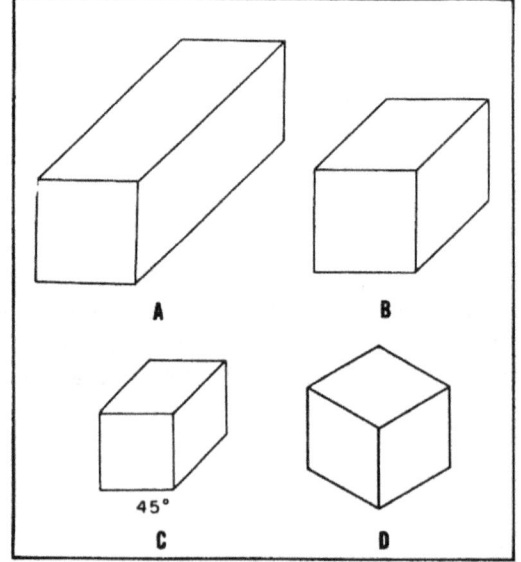

Figure 3-13. A. Cavalier drawing. B. Cabinet drawing. C. Oblique drawing. C. Isometric drawing

SPECIAL VIEWS

In many complex objects it is often difficult for the draftsmen to show true size and shapes of an object orthographically. Therefore, the draftsmen must use other media to give the engineer and craftsman a clear picture of the object to be constructed. Among these media are auxiliary views, rotations, details, section views, phantom views, exploded views, and developments. These special views will be covered in this chapter.

AUXILIARY VIEWS

Auxiliary views are often necessary to clearly show the true shape and length of inclined surfaces, or other features which are not parallel to any of the principal planes of projection.

Look directly at the front view of Figure 3-14. Notice the inclined surface. Now look at the right side view and top view. The inclined surface appears foreshortened—not its true shape or size. For a case like this, the draftsman will use the auxiliary view to show the true shape and size of the inclined face of the object. It is obtained by looking directly at the inclined surface. The principle of the auxiliary view is illustrated in Figure 3-15.

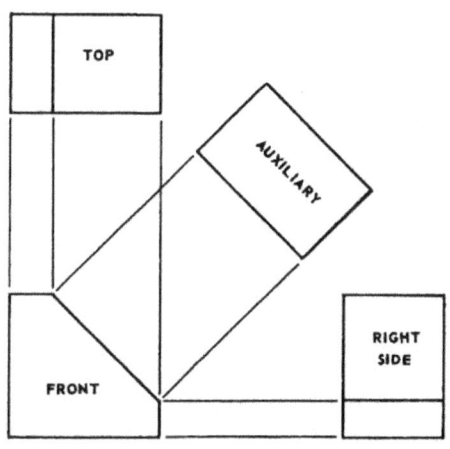

Figure 3-14. Auxiliary view arrangement.

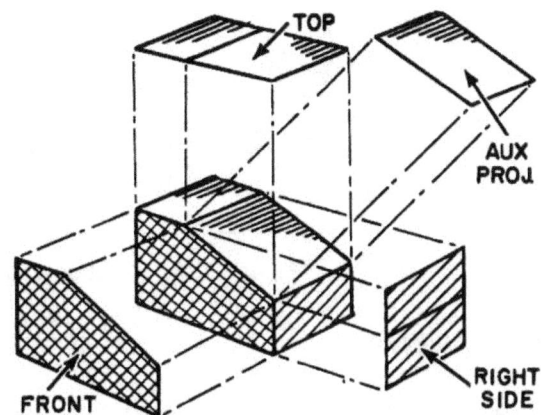

Figure 3-15. Auxiliary projection principle.

If you would reflect for a moment back to Figure 3-5 showing the immovable object being viewed from the front, top, and side to obtain the three orthographic views, and compare it with Figure 3-16, together with the other information, it should clearly explain the reading of the auxiliary view. For a side by side comparison of an orthographic view and an auxiliary projection, see Figure 3-17. You will see a foreshortened orthographic view in Figure 3-17a of the inclined or slanted surface whose true size and shape are shown in Figure 3-17b.

Figure 3-16. Viewing an inclined surface. auxiliary view.

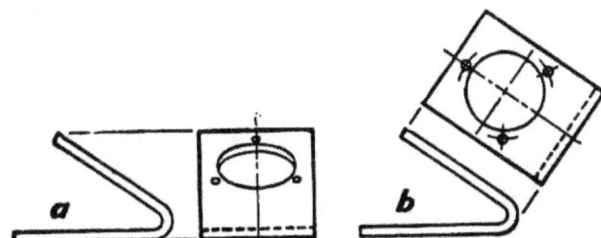

Figure 3-17. Comparison of orthographic and auxiliary projection.

ROTATION

The projection of the auxiliary view as mentioned earlier is obtained by the observer moving around an immovable object, and the views projected perpendicular to the lines of sight. Remember, the object has not been moved, only the position of the viewer has changed.

In a rotation view the object is moved (rotated), while the viewer remains stationary.

Figure 3-18 illustrates a 2-view orthographic view (A), an auxiliary view (B), and a rotation view (C) of an object. To clarify the rotation principle, an extra top view has been inserted (circled) to show the object rotated on its center axis and the right portion, from the center line of the object, has been projected in the front view. In short, the rotation view is similar to taking the auxiliary view (B), and placing it horizontally against the front view (B).

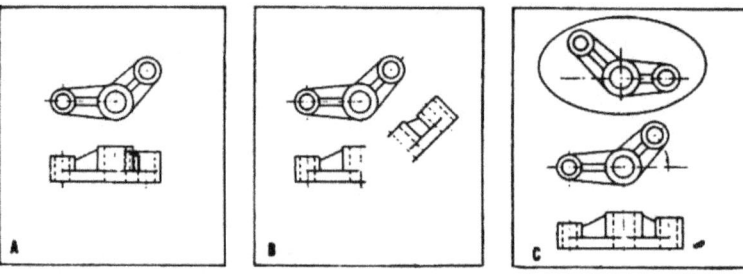

Figure 3-18. Rotation and auxiliary views compared.

PHANTOM VIEWS

Phantom views are used to indicate the alternate position of parts of the item drawn, repeated detail, or the relative position of an absent part. Figure 3-19 shows a phantom view of a part in the alternate position (the part to the left of the figure made up one long line and two short dashes).

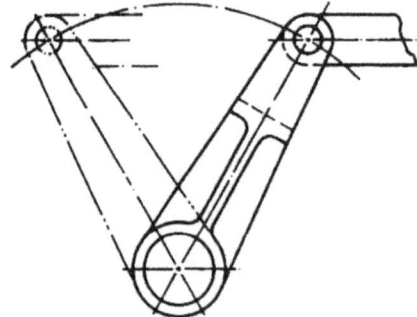

Figure 3-19. Phantom view showing alternative position.

SECTIONS

Section views are used to give a clearer view of the interior or hidden feature of an object which normally cannot be clearly observed in conventional outside views.

A section view is obtained by cutting away part of an object to show the shape and construction at the cutting plane.

Notice the cutting plane line AA in Figure 3-20A. It shows where the imaginary cut has been made. The isometric view in Figure 3-20B helps you to visualize the cutting plane. The arrows point in the direction in which you are to look at the sectional view.

Figure 3-20C is a front showing how the object would look if it were cut in half.

The orthographic section view of Section A-A, Figure 3-20D, is placed on the drawing instead of the confusing front view in Figure 3-20A. Notice how much easier it is to read and understand.

When sectional views are drawn, the part that is cut by the cutting plane is marked with diagonal, parallel section lines. The draftsmen's word for the process of making these lines is crosshatching. When two or more parts are shown in one view, each part is sectioned or crosshatched with a different slant of line. Section views are necessary for a clear understanding of complicated parts. On simple drawings, a section may serve the purpose of an additional view.

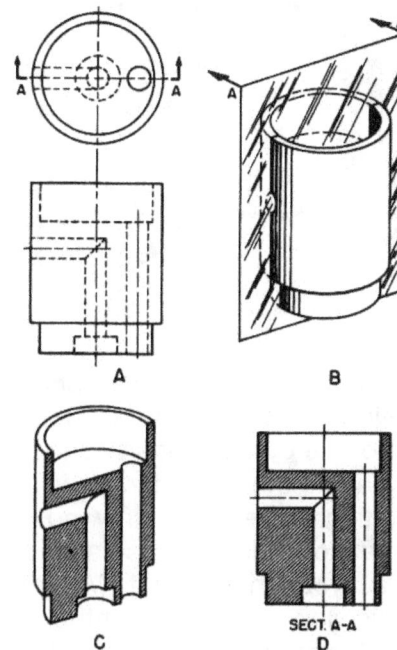

Figure 3-20. Action of a cutting plane.

OFFSET SECTION

A section view which has the cutting plane changing direction backward and forward (zig-zag), so as to pass through features that are important to show, is known as an offset section. The offset cutting plane in Figure 3-21 is arranged so that the hole on the right side will be shown in section. The sectional view is the front view, and the top views show the offset cutting plane line.

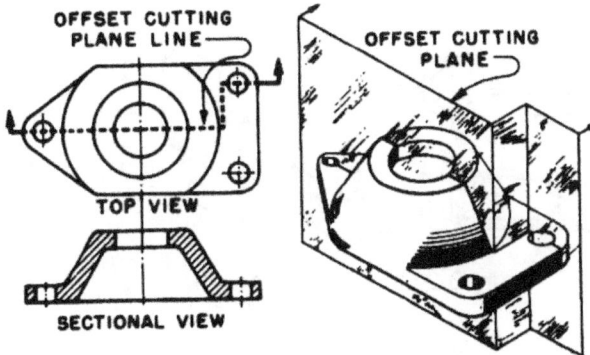

Figure 3-21. Offset section.

HALF SECTION

Figure 3-22 shows a half section. A half section is normally used when the object is symmetrical in both outside and inside details. One-half of the object is sectioned; the outer half is shown as a standard view.

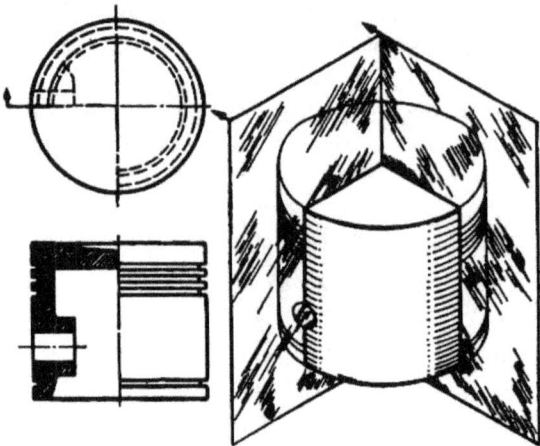

Figure 3-22. Half section.

The object is round, and if it were cut into two equal parts and then those parts divided equally, you would have four quarters. Now remove a quarter. This is what the cutting plane has done in the pictorial view. A quarter of the cylinder has been removed so that you can look inside. If the cutting plane had extended along the diameter of the cylinder, you would have been looking at a full section. But the cutting plane in this drawing extends the distance of the radius, or only half the distance of a full section. Hence, it is called a half section.

The arrow has been inserted to show your line of sight. What you see from that point is drawn as a half section in the orthographic view. The width of the orthographic view represents the diameter of the circle. One radius is shown as a half section, the other as an external view.

REVOLVED SECTION

To eliminate drawing extra views of rolled shapes, ribs, and similar forms, the draftsman uses a revolved section. It is really a drawing within a drawing, and it clearly describes the object's shape at a certain cross-section station or point.

The draftsman has revolved the sectional view of the rib in Figure 3-23 so that you can look at it head-on. Because of this revolving feature, this kind of section is called a revolved section.

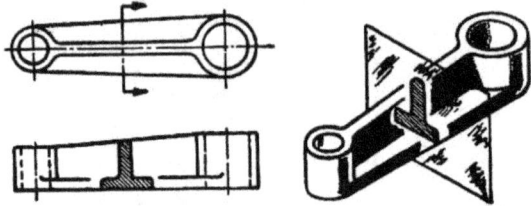

Figure 3-23. Revolved section.

REMOVED SECTION

Removed sections are normally used to illustrate particular parts of an object. They are drawn like the revolved section, except that they are placed at one side to bring out important details. They are often drawn to a larger scale than the view on which they are indicated (Figure 3-24).

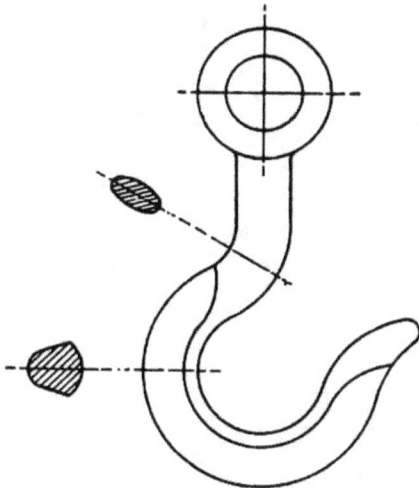

Figure 3-24. Removed section.

BROKEN OUT SECTION

The inner structure of a small area may be shown by peeling back or removing the outside surface. The inside of the counterbored hole is better illustrated in Figure 3-25 because of the broken-out section, which makes it possible for you to "look inside."

Figure 3-25. Broken-out section through a counterbored hole.

ALIGNED SECTION

Look at the front view of the handwheel in Figure 3-26. Notice the cutting plane line AA.
When a true sectional view might be misleading, parts such as ribs or spokes are drawn as if they are rotated into or out of the cutting plane. Notice that the spokes in the section at A-A ae not sectioned. In some cases, though not in this figure, if the spokes were sectioned, the first impression would be that the wheel had a solid web rather than spokes.

32

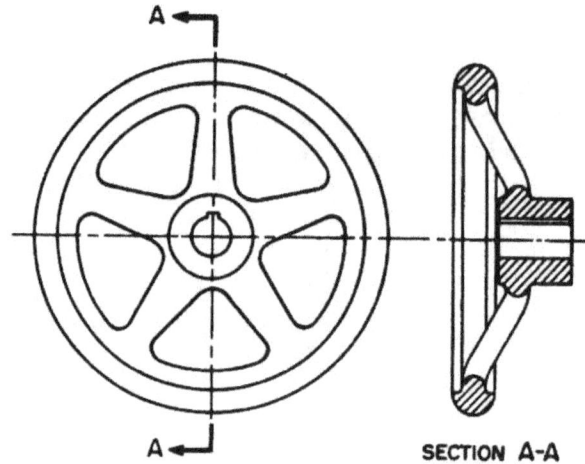

Figure 3-26. Aligned section.

EXPLODED VIEWS

Another special type of view, which is very helpful and easy to read, is the exploded view. The exploded view is used to show relative location of parts; it is particularly helpful in assembling complex objects. Notice how parts are spread out in line to show clearly each part's relationship to the other parts (Figure 3-27).

Figure 3-27. An exploded view.

DEVELOPMENTS

Development is the method a layout man uses to make a flat pattern which can be transferred to sheet metal and formed into a curved or angular form. The Shipfitter (M) and the Steelworker (F) do a great deal of this but men of most ratings will benefit by knowing even a little something about development from a blueprint reading point of view.

In Figure 3-28A you will see a pictorial view of a sheet metal cone. As the cone has no bottom, we can look into it and see the joint which has purposely been left open for this illustration. To find out how the development or pattern for this cone would look, see Figure 3-28B. The length of the side of the cone (not the height from base to top) is represented on the development as L. The circumference of the base of the cone is represented by the curved dimension line and the letter C. The stretchout, B, in the figure (stretchout is another name used interchangeably with pattern or development), when rolled up, would give you the cone shown in A. Likewise, you could transfer the stretchout to sheet metal, run the metal through a slip roll forming machine, and you would have a sheet metal cone.

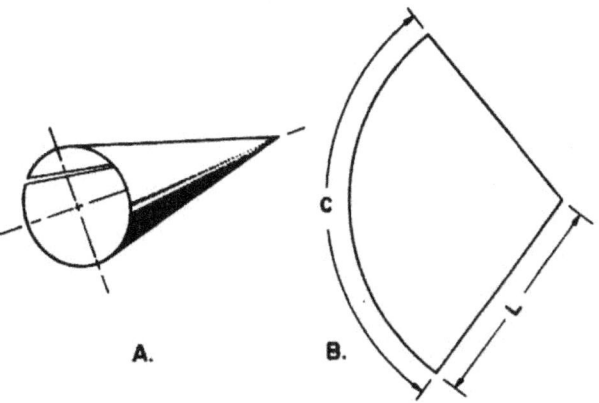

Figure 3-28. Sheet metal cone.

ANSWERS TO QUESTION ON JIG BLOCK

1. 1 ½"
2. 2"
3. 3 1/2"
4. h
5. Outline or visible lines
6. N
7. T
8. 1"
9. ½"
10. Dimension lines
11. Extension lines
12. M
13. G
14. 1"
15. 2"
16. U
17. L
18. 7
19. Cold rolled steel
20. S and P
21. J, K, and L